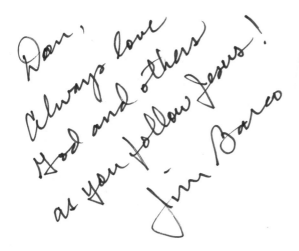

Dan,
Always love
God and others
as you follow Jesus!
Jim Barco

# Excel in Your World

## James Barco

Gazelle
PRESS

*Excel in Your World*
by James Barco
Copyright ©2012 James Barco

ISBN 978-1-58169-423-9
For Worldwide Distribution
Printed in the U.S.A.

Gazelle Press
P.O. Box 191540 • Mobile, AL 36619
800-367-8203

# Table of Contents

# Introduction

Indeed, man wishes to be happy even when he so lives as to make happiness impossible. —*St. Augustine*

All of us long for a rewarding and fulfilling life, in other words, a happy life. Jesus described such a life when He declared in John 10:10, "I have come that they may have life, and have it to the full." How can we have a life like this and avoid making happiness impossible? Since we will not get much assistance from a world that is unfriendly to Christian values, *Excel in Your World* is designed to help us find the full life Jesus promised. We do not have to be at the mercy of belief systems that have no place for God.

As these ideas are identified, it will help us understand the forces that work against having the life Jesus promised. Learning the biblical template or framework provided in this book will help to counteract the influences of a secular world. Discovering that we are part of the grand design that God has for this world lifts us to a higher plane of living. And grasping the big picture of what God is doing to establish His kingdom principles enables us to understand how our daily lives fit into His broader plans. He has invited us to be a part of the glory of what He is doing to redeem the world.

As we study the words that Jesus spoke to the Sadducees in Matthew 22:34-40, the firm foundation of love can be established on which to build our lives. It will be challenging to change the way that we think, but the rewards will be enormous as we learn to focus on the things that are truly important.

The journey to the full life which Jesus offers will enhance every area of our lives. They will be reshaped as we learn to use God's pattern. Marriages and families will be strengthened even as we are confronted by a secular world that thinks it has discovered a better model. Churches will become more relevant and productive. The work world will take on new dimensions for us.

These and many other areas are discussed in this book to assist us with how to apply the teachings of Jesus. As we move out of our comfort zones of easy Christianity we will hear a needy world crying out for someone to help them and care about them. Repentance, God's grace, and forgiveness in Christ will keep us moving forward on our spiritual journey to love God and others. It will keep us on the path to excel in our world when we stumble in our walk with God.

One book like this is too short and life is too complex to answer all our questions. Since God deals with us as individuals, we can make use of the framework provided in this book to find the answers needed for daily living. It will take commitment and discipline on our part to pray and study the Bible regularly. We may rest assured God has the guidance needed to live for Him.

More can be learned by reading other books that delve in greater detail into specific topics. Surrounding ourselves with a community of believers will make our journey a lot richer as we link hands with friends who are headed in the same direction.

First Corinthians 14:8 says, "If the trumpet does not sound a clear call, who will get ready for battle?" There are many confusing voices competing for our allegiance today. We need a clear sound to follow. *Excel in Your World* seeks to provide that clear sound.

1

# The Challenge

"To every man there openeth
A way, and ways, and a way.
And the high soul climbs the high way,
And the low soul the low,
And in between on the misty flats,
The rest drift to and fro.
But to every man there openeth
A high way and a low;
And every man decideth
Which way his soul shall go."
—*John Oxenham, "The Ways"*

Carrie had done her weekly grocery shopping. When she entered her car, she checked her receipt and noticed a package of meat had been missed by the check-out clerk. She had a brief discussion with herself. Should she just drive home and forget it? After all, the store would never know the difference. Since Carrie was a believer, she decided to return and tell the store about the mistake.

Many people would not say Carrie's decision was a standard of excellence. Some would even think her foolish. She did not discover a cure for cancer, make millions at business, or become a tennis star at Wimbledon, England. She made a simple moral decision based on her values as a Christian. While many would not understand her choice, Carrie's decision was indeed a mark of moral and ethical excellence.

We make decisions like this all the time. Making wise decisions that lead to excellence is the challenge we face as believers every day. What can we use as our guide when we buy a car, change jobs, attend college, vote in an election, or put a parent in a nursing home? What goes through our minds at work or in the supermarket?

## The Danger Zone

Donald G. Barnhouse tells an interesting story of errand boys who traveled the streets of London whistling as they went about their work. An alert musician noticed the boys were whistling off key. After investigating, he discovered the bells of Westminster Abbey were ringing slightly out of tune. The boys were just copying what they heard every day. This is a picture of what is happening in the current generation of Christians. Too many of us are off pitch in our lives because we have been affected by an ungodly world around us.

Unfortunately, the average Christian today has been described as being captured by our culture. This leaves them, as Oxenham has described, "in between on the misty flats" to "drift to and fro." Too many of us make daily decisions based, not on what the Bible teaches, but on what our culture teaches us and what our sinful nature desires. We have allowed the idea of the good life to be defined by what is bigger, better, and newer, not by what is pleasing to God.

Like the weathering of rocks in a hillside stream, a slow but steady process is eroding the Christian faith in our hearts and minds. The clash of secular world views or belief systems with a biblical world view is unrelenting. Listening to an off key world has left too many of us unprepared and missing in action. This is a major issue facing us in our world. It raises ominous warning signs about the future of Christianity in our modern western culture.

A look at the decline of Christianity in Europe should alert us to what is happening in the United States. Europe was the birthplace of the Protestant Reformation. Missionaries were sent to all parts of the world. However, church attendance has dropped precipitously. Islam is on the rise. It is ironic that today, missionaries are being sent to Europe.

Unfortunately, many are unaware that we are headed in the same direction in the United States unless we change course. We can reverse this downward spiral if we allow God to change us into a people who seek moral excellence.

What is happening to cause this shift away from biblical values? While the answer is complex, one of the major contributing causes is our limited biblical knowledge. This creates a lack of understanding of and commitment to a godly way of life. Briefly stated, many Christians do not know how to use kingdom principles to live a Christian lifestyle.

Sadly, some churches are failing to provide the teaching needed to live a God inspired life in our world. A survey was made of 4,000 laymen in 114 evangelical churches across the United States. One question asked was, "Do you feel the preaching on Sunday relates to what's going on in your life?" Over 83% saw virtually no connection between what they heard on Sunday morning and what they faced on Monday morning.[1] Equally disturbing is that many of us fail to take advantage of good teaching when it is offered. It is in this context that the understanding of biblical living in this book is offered.

Wouldn't it be wonderful if we had a pill or could insert a computer chip in our brains to give us instant biblical knowledge? We all know this is not going to happen. It has to be done the old fashioned way. It takes work; it takes the exercise of our minds to learn what the Bible teaches about the basics of godly living.

Billy Graham was once asked, "If you had to live your life over again, what would you do differently?" His surprising answer was, "One of my great regrets is that I have not studied enough. I wish I had studied more and preached less."[2]

Learning to live a godly life requires some spiritual elbow grease. Our friend, Carrie, did not make her decision in a vacuum. She obviously had put forth the effort to learn honesty and integrity. Paul's words in 2 Timothy 2:15 are still relevant to us, "Do your best to present yourself to God as one approved, a workman who does not need to be ashamed and who correctly handles the word of truth."

## Confronting the Problem

Our challenge is to learn to live the way God wants us to live, to move from "in between on the misty flats" to a clear understanding of His principles for living and then climb to "the high way" of God. Jesus taught us in Matthew 7:13-14, "Enter through the narrow gate. For wide is the gate and broad is the road that leads to destruction, and many enter through it. But small is the gate and narrow is the road that leads to life, and only a few find it." Our culture offers us the wide gate and the easy, broad road. Entering the small gate and traveling the narrow road will require us to learn a way of life that will be at odds with the world.

Learning to live a God-inspired life is not just an intellectual process. A. W. Tozer once said, "Unused truth becomes as useless as an unused muscle." God's truth must penetrate to the core of our being, our hearts. It needs to be done in the crucible of our daily relationships and the ups and downs of life. It will require a change in our attitudes and our lifestyles. And it needs to be done in the real world where it will not always be neat and tidy.

The call to live by kingdom principles is not a call to an easy path. It will challenge us on many levels. The mistakes we make will be part of the process of learning and growing. The removal of sinful ideas, bad attitudes, and ungodly behavior may be painful at times.

Entering the small gate and walking the narrow road will demand perseverance and persistence. Support will be needed from fellow believers on this journey. It is important to be in close contact with a small group of believers where support and prayer can be received when the going gets tough. Our commitment to follow Jesus will then be strengthened by the company of others. We cannot change ourselves or our world on our own. Building God's kingdom is a group endeavor.

A big, soft easy chair is great for relaxing. It's so comfortable that we don't want to leave it. But we can become like that as believers. We must avoid the mistake of limiting the Christian life to the easy routines of attending church and believing the right doctrines. Jesus did not call His disciples to a comfortable lifestyle in the suburbs of Jerusalem.

After we have read our Bibles and prayed, we need to enter the real world and use what we have learned of God and His grace in Christ to impact those around us. Like Carrie, we shop and live in neighborhoods, work in jobs, and send our children to school. As we do that, we can carry with us the commitment to live a godly life and apply the kingdom principles of our Lord in our daily endeavors. Individually and collectively we can change the status quo and remove from our hearts and minds the cloud of ignorance and the spiritual impotence that threaten our resolve.

We do not have to be great spiritual giants to rise to the challenge of living a life of moral excellence. This is a myth which falls far short of reality. Thomas Merton stated, "It is in the ordinary duties and labors of life that the Christian can and should develop his spiritual union with God."

The Bible is filled with flawed, ordinary people like the twelve disciples who chose to change the direction of their lives. No special aura surrounded them as they used the common activities of daily living to be God's light in a dark world. Their efforts continue today like ever spreading ripples in a pond. When we add up the little things of our everyday lives, their importance becomes impressive and extraordinary. The quality of our lives will speak volumes to others, one day at a time.

Getting our lives on pitch with biblical principles will earn us the right to make a difference in a broken world drifting "in between on the misty flats." This is our challenge as believers. As we seek God's "high way" and allow Him to change us, we can be used to change our world. As we embrace the challenge of excelling in our world, we must not underestimate the power and influence our lives can have for God.

[1]Howard Hendricks, 1984 Multnomah Pastor's Enrichment Conference
[2]*Christianity Today,* September 12, 1977, p. 19.

## Further study, reflection, or discussion:

1. Use a scale of 1 (low) to 10 (high) to answer the following questions.
2. How do the teachings of the Bible affect you in your daily decision making?
3. How would you rate your knowledge of what the Bible teaches about godly living?
4. How would you rate your effort at learning what the Bible teaches about godly living?
5. How would you rate your influence for God as a believer on your family, friends, neighbors and co-workers?

2

# What Happened in Bible Times?

*I am the Lord your God, who brought you out of Egypt, out of the land of slavery. You shall have no other gods before me* (Exodus 20:2-3).

Solomon had a great start to his reign as king of Israel. He had survived the family feuds of his brothers to succeed his father, David. He had inherited a strong and stable country, and he was now wealthy. He prayed and God gave him wisdom. 1 Kings 4:29 describes his wisdom as a "very great insight and a breadth of understanding as measureless as the sand on the seashore." His advice was sought by many people as well as surrounding kings. Even the queen of Sheba paid him a visit. He distinguished himself in Israel by building the first temple in Jerusalem. Solomon seemed to have it all.

But despite his wisdom and accomplishments, 1 Kings 11:4-6 tells us,

*As Solomon grew old, his wives turned his heart after other gods, and his heart was not fully devoted to the Lord his God, as the heart of David his father had been. He followed Ashtoreth the goddess of the Sidonians, and Molech the detestable god of the Ammonites. So Solomon did evil in the eyes of the Lord; he did not follow the Lord completely, as David his father had done.*

Solomon began his reign well, yet near the end of his life he strayed from God because he was under the influence of his wives who worshipped the foreign gods of his day. His sad ending illustrates the struggle the Israelites had with the influence of an ungodly world throughout their history in the Old Testament. They failed to live by the standards of moral excellence that God had given them through Moses.

## Old Testament Challenges

Having lived in Egypt for several generations, the Israelites had a firsthand knowledge of the gods of the Egyptians. This influence followed them on their journey to the Promised Land even as God revealed His law to them through Moses. They struggled right from the start, continually grumbling and complaining to Moses as they wandered in the desert.

When Moses was on the mountain receiving the law from God, his brother Aaron made a golden calf. When he returned, he found the people dancing and cavorting in revelry before it. Moses, in anger, threw the tablets of stone, shattering them on the ground. Moses knew that the first command given by God was clear, "You shall have no other gods before me."

They were warned later in Deuteronomy 18:9-13,

*When you enter the land the Lord your God is giving you, do not learn to imitate the detestable ways of the nations there. Let no one be found among you who sacrifices his son or daughter in the fire, who practices divination or sorcery, interprets omens, engages in witchcraft, or casts spells, or who is a medium or spiritist or who consults the dead. Anyone who does these things is detestable to the Lord, and because of these detestable practices the Lord your God will drive out those nations before. You must be blameless before the Lord your God.*

Unfortunately, it did not take long for the Israelites to disobey Moses' warning. Judges 2:10-13 tells us,

*After that whole generation had been gathered to their fathers, another generation grew up, who knew neither the Lord nor what he had done for Israel. Then the Israelites did evil in the eyes of the Lord and served the Baals. They forsook the Lord, the God of their fathers, who had brought then out of Egypt. They followed and worshiped various gods of the people around them. They provoked the Lord to anger because they forsook him and served Baal and the Ashtoreths.*

These Canaanite gods and goddesses became major obstacles to the Jews as they lived in the land that God had given them. Failing to keep Moses' instructions caused a spiritual roller coaster ride of ups and downs to occur. These were characterized by long periods of rebellion as the Jews pursued the gods of their neighbors, some of whom practiced temple prostitution and even child sacrifice. Elijah's confrontation with King Ahab and the prophets of Baal on Mount Carmel in 1 Kings 18 is one of the classic and dramatic stories illustrating this spiritual struggle.

The Old Testament prophets cataloged the sins of the Israelites generation after generation. Their books provide a social commentary on the moral failure of the nation. Time and again a heavy price was paid for the disobedience and rebellion of the Jewish people. Finally, they were removed from the land and taken into captivity. The northern ten tribes of Israel were taken into exile by the Assyrians. Later the southern kingdom was taken captive by the Babylonians.

The story of Israel in the Old Testament gives us many lessons. It warns of the dangerous influences of an ungodly culture and how that can lead to moral failure. It demonstrates the tendency of human nature to seek its own way. It clearly shows how far and how fast people can stray from God's ways. And it illustrates the steep price to be paid when God's principles are forsaken. All these failures teach us the necessity of training our children in the ways of the Lord and demonstrate how each successive generation must choose to follow Him.

## New Testament Challenges

The New Testament provides an account in the Book of Acts of a young emerging church encountering all kinds of challenges. They were grappling with growth and struggling with the tensions between Christian Jews and the Gentiles who wanted to become followers of Christ. These tensions and problems did not take long to develop.

Acts 8 tells of the Samaritans receiving Christ when Philip proclaimed the gospel to them. Acts 10 details Peter's encounter with Cornelius, the Roman centurion. Acts 11 describes the discussion over the issue of Gentiles believing in Christ. This shift from the Jews to the Gentiles is dramatically depicted in Acts 13:46. Paul and Barnabus replied to the Jews at Pisidian Antioch, "We had to speak the word of God to you first. Since you rejected it and do not consider yourselves worthy of eternal life, we now turn to the Gentiles."

Acts 15 records the great council at Jerusalem that resolved the issue of whether Gentiles had to follow the Law of Moses. The latter part of Acts deals with Paul's outreach to the Mediterranean world and the influx of those who were raised in the surrounding religions of that day. The epistles are sprinkled with references to conflicts and issues that arose as Gentiles became followers of Christ.

Paul's travels and contact with the religious world of his day gave him a wide look at the results of their beliefs and practices. He gave this uncompromising assessment of his day in Romans 1:21-23. "For although they knew God, they neither glorified him as God nor gave thanks to him, but their thinking became futile and their foolish hearts were darkened. Although they claimed to be wise, they became fools and exchanged the glory of the immortal God for images made to look like mortal man and birds and animals and reptiles." He concluded in verse 32, "Although they know God's righteous decree that those who do such things deserve death, they not only continue to do these very things but also approve of those who practice them."

Paul looked at his world and concluded that it was at serious odds with the Christian life. He devoted his life to helping the believers of his time learn to live by the kingdom principles of Christ. His letters are filled with instructions on godly living as well as warnings about the dangerous beliefs that would change and corrupt the Gospel of Christ.

Particularly interesting are the letters that John wrote to the seven churches in Revelation 2 and 3. The words to the Ephesus church in Revelation 2:4 warn, "You have forsaken your first love." The church in Pergamum received a stinging indictment in 2:15 for having "those who hold to the teaching of the Nicolaitans."

The church in Thyatira was criticized in 2:20, "You tolerate that woman Jezebel, who calls herself a prophetess." The church in Sardis was told in 3:1, "You have a reputation of being alive, but you are dead." The church in Laodicea was sternly rebuked in 3:15-16, "I know your deeds, that you are neither cold nor hot. I wish you were either one or the other! So, because you are lukewarm—neither cold nor hot—I am about to spit you out of my mouth." These problems did not develop in a vacuum but in a culture that had eroded their Christian values.

The history of the Israelites provides many insights into their struggles to remain faithful to God. Their story gives us striking examples of success and failure in that effort. Paul's assessment in Romans gives an alarming description that is, in an uncanny way, accurate to our day. The letters to the seven churches in Revelation still resonate and pose relevant questions to the church. These same problems and tensions have continued down through church history and are with us today.

We also are confronted by a godless world that is not friendly to Christian values. Our challenge is still the same as it was in Bible times. How do we recognize the gods of our day? As believers, what principles are we to use to excel in our world? How vital it is to find answers to these and other questions!

## Further study, reflection, and discussion:

1. Use a Bible dictionary to study the following pagan gods and goddesses: Asherah, Ashtoreth, Baal, Chemosh, Dagon, and Molech. See also high places.
2. Do an internet search to study Roman gods and goddesses.
3. Review the results of Israel's idolatry in 2 Kings 17:7-23.
4. How does Psalm 106 portray the nation of Israel?
5. Review the events and issues of the Jerusalem Council in Acts 15.
6. What happened to Paul in Acts 19:23-41?
7. What did Paul say about eating meat offered to idols in 1 Corinthians 8:1-13?
8. Review the lessons and warnings Paul gave in 1 Corinthians 10:1-33.

3

# What's Happening in Our World?

*Men have forgotten God: that's why all this has happened.*
*—Aleksandr Solzhenitsyn*

Several years ago a Boy Scout troop visited the National Zoo in Washington D.C. only to be shocked when they were denied the use of a public facility. The Smithsonian, which owns the zoo, ruled the Boy Scouts organization is biased because members are required to believe in God. Religious expression in public places was not to be permitted. Thankfully this ruling was later overturned.

One major city renamed Christmas as "sparkle season." A local school district changed Easter Eggs to "spring ovals."[1] This attitude to suppress things Christian occurs with increasing frequency. Our country once was thought to be a Christian nation. What has changed? After all, our country was founded on Judeo-Christian principles. While this may have been true in the past, we are fast developing a secular way of life.

While idols are not worshipped as in biblical times, we are still being strongly influenced by non-Christian belief systems that control our lives. This often occurs without us being aware of what is happening. Though not as obvious, these ideas rise to the level of a secular religion. It is vitally important for us to be alerted to these forces and the way they shape our culture and our individual lives.

Bill O'Reilly from *Fox News* often talks and writes about those he calls secular-progressives.[2] Who are these people? O'Reilly tells us that they are left-wing liberals with a social/political agenda who like to call themselves progressives. Though some appear religious, their philosophical roots can be traced to secular humanism and naturalism, which deny the existence of the supernatural.

Progressives are those with a liberal view of the world. They have been influenced by two competing belief systems that have shaped our way of life for many years. These ideas run much deeper and are far more widespread than most of us think.

## Modernism

The older of these belief systems is modernism.[3] A quick summary reveals modernists would have us believe the only path to knowledge is through reason and the scientific method. Truth in the spiritual and moral realms is only a matter of our personal convictions. Therefore, it says we should cast aside the teachings of religion, primarily the outdated Judeo-Christian heritage. We are told mankind is basically good and can use the powers of reason and ingenuity to solve all worldly problems. Man is the measure of all things and can develop a higher and more up-to-date morality.

We will be led to a better world and personal happiness by scientific discovery, technology, education, and economic advancement. As the world moves toward this utopia the motto will be: "We can save the world." After all, modernists know what is best and proclaim it with religious fervor. Unfortunately, these well-intended attempts by modernists to save the world have not turned out as hoped. The failures of following these ideas have left many of us skeptical and disillusioned.

## Postmodernism

A more recent belief system impacting us is called post-modernism.[4] This is a secular reaction to modernism's arrogance, dreams of a utopia, and the illusion of human progress. The failures we have experienced following modernism fuel this backlash.

Post-modernists tell us to reject objective truth. Since we cannot separate ourselves from the process of interpretation, what we think to be true is tainted by the very process of our attempt to interpret. All truth is subjective; therefore, you can have your truth and I can have my truth. We also need to be skeptical and suspicious of any authority. Since written history is only an attempt to impose order on past events, we are not to believe anything we are told.

It further states that personal experience is the only way to true understanding. Therefore, our authority is from within. Since all faiths share a common origin, traditional authorities like Christianity and Judaism are to be pushed aside. We must make way for other truths under the banners of tolerance and multiculturalism.

We also have an evolving self and identity. Like an onion, just peel away the layers of experience and discover ourselves. Assume any identity or lifestyle. Our response to ethical questions is, "Only if it works for me."

The words of this woman speak volumes: "I feel I'm faithful to Christianity, but I've done some things that people around me, I guess, would consider immoral, sinful, and they still have trouble embracing the things I've done. In fact, I don't think my mother visits me too much because I'm living in a situation in which I'm not married and stuff like that. But I don't share her views on that, and I know her views are rooted in her religion. But it doesn't work for me that way."[5]

Following postmodernism also produces certain unintended consequences. It teeters on the brink of anarchy. Openness to all ideas consequently creates a state of not knowing and potential meaningless. The onion has no core. This leads to an "anything goes" approach to a life filled with uncertainty, anxiety, and a constant quest for something to fill the God hole in our lives.

## The Impact in Our World

Let's look further at the impact these belief systems have on various areas of our daily life. A brief look reveals the problems spread across the broad spectrum of our culture. The high sounding ideas of the secular intellectuals have again left us with unintended consequences in the real world.

One of the key areas to be affected is the morality that guides us as individuals and gives us a civil society. Modernists tell us to reject the supernatural and any morality identified as being spiritual. Those who are committed to the traditional Judeo-Christian way of life are seen as repressive and no longer relevant today. Those who hold to traditional values are the new enemies of progress.

We have seen how liberals tell us we are capable of creating a better morality. All we have to do is redefine what was once considered evil. Former bad behavior is declared no longer evil but the results of society's ignorance. The key is to educate ourselves with the new morality. The results have cascaded through our culture like an ever widening torrent.

As multiculturalism is emphasized, every culture is seen as morally equal. Criticism of another culture is deemed intolerant. This is what happened when, on April 22, 2010, the Pentagon rescinded Franklin Graham's invitation to speak at a Pentagon National Day of Prayer event. He had been publicly critical of Islam in an interview with Campbell Brown on CNN on December 11, 2009.[6] Graham's comments were cherry picked by our media. His supporting comments were left out. Those who declare that Jesus is the way, the truth, and the life, are deemed intolerant like Franklin Graham as well.

The arts are windows into the soul of our culture. They have become the visible and audible showcases for this new morality. Objective art has been replaced with the subjective where anything goes. Have you noticed that some music sounds like noise? This is because the musicians have rejected the balanced sounds of traditional music for the clash of atonal sounds that are little more than noise. The coarsening of our culture assaults our eyes and ears every day. Shock, anti-art and music lyrics are meant to offend the old morality.

Art is whatever the artist declares it to be. Even critics can no longer tell what art is. Several years ago a watercolor painting named *Rhythm of the Trees* won an art competition. Judges described it as having "a certain quality of color balance, composition, and technical skill." The painting was actually done by a four-year old child. The mother had submitted it as a joke.[7] It seems that now even our pets and animals can create valuable works of art.

Economics reveal a confusion of ideas about how to spend the public's money. The national debt as of June 2011 topped 14.4 trillion dollars. Keynesian economics, emphasizing the roll of the federal government spending in economic stimulation, have helped lead us to this point. Millions are out of work. However, we rebel when our share of federal generosity is threatened. A "what's-in-it-for-me" mentality occupies the thinking of many.

We hear daily about the political posturing and the pandering to constituent groups that creates gridlock in making changes to local, state, and federal budgets. Some assume that more government spending is the solution to economic problems. An even greater problem of limited government resources looms like a dark cloud of uncertainty on our horizon.

Education is another battleground in our society. The United States now ranks eighteenth among thirty-six developed nations. Old instructional methods that educated most of us have been replaced with what we are assured are more enlightened models. Moral freedom from old ideas is to be the goal. Our children now can attend classes teaching a variety of ideas about feminism and alternative lifestyles.

Traditional morality has given way to values clarification where our children are encouraged to develop their own ideas about right and wrong. Parental values are often contradicted. After all, the experts tell us that our children are basically good and can figure things out for themselves. Is it any wonder that cheating and plagiarism are rampant? The new freedom in educational goals is having disastrous and unintended consequences. What will happen when our children become adults?

Our legal system has been impacted enormously by these world views. Judicial activism has been a major source of laws that have redefined our country, by-passing elected officials. This is how abortion was legalized in 1973. Over 53 million lives have been aborted since then.

The constitutional provision of the separation of church and state has been used to remove all religious sayings and symbols from our public places. Case after case has struck down the place that the morals of our Judeo-Christian heritage once held in our society. We are not allowed to post The Ten

Commandments on public buildings. Crosses are routinely prohibited on publically owned land. The teaching of creationism and the argument from design have been forbidden in our children's public classrooms. Case law setting precedents for future laws in our country is growing daily reflecting the liberal agenda.

Politics is another arena where the battle for our minds rages. The previous paragraphs list a number of areas where secular minded politicians have sided with liberal judges and passed laws contrary to our beliefs. Christians running for office are marked and attacked for having extreme views that are out of touch with the mainstream of society.

We are told legislation must be accomplished by what is called the "art of compromise." Cherished morals must be sacrificed at times to make opposing groups happy. Principle gives way to what some hope will work, which in the end may not work. We have seen numerous bad laws enacted with equally bad results. The war on poverty was passed under President Lyndon Johnson. Charles Colson has astutely observed, "Well, today the war is over, and poverty won."[8]

Science and medicine continue to struggle with a lack of moral direction in the effort to find cures for many illnesses and physical problems. Gene manipulation has given rise to this hope. While there have been positive results, we need to note the key is in the definition of what is unwanted. Already this is being applied to the abortion of children who are deemed undesirable. Scientists are now talking of creating made-to-order children.

Stem cell research is also touted as having tremendous benefits for cures of our injuries and disease. Even though stem cells may be harvested from several sources, the use of embryonic cells from human embryos at the first stages of life is used to develop these cures. Our culture lacks the moral foundation to keep up with these and other scientific developments.

Social problems continue to plague us on a daily basis. Unfortunately, the foundation for these problems has been laid by secular progressives who reject traditional values in favor of the self-determined morals of those who claim to know best.

When we are taught and allowed to determine our own values, the results are obvious—society begins to disintegrate. This contradicts the liberal's belief in the basic goodness of man. The recent development of flash mobs of youths rampaging in our cities is a clear signal. Poverty, the war on drugs, crime, and other social ills continue. So far, drugs, street crime, prostitution, corporate crime, and the like are winning.

Sadly, it is our families that have taken a terrible blow in the search for a newer, better morality. The divorce rate today is a commentary on our concept of what it means to be married. Many couples get married today without any idea of how to live together. Census data reveals less than 48 percent of households in the United States are occupied by a traditional husband and wife.

One little girl in school was asked by a classmate who the man was with her mother. She replied that it was her daddy. The classmate shot back, "No. Daddies don't live with mommies."[9] It is the children who must bear the burden of family dysfunction.

The family as we have known it is rapidly changing right before our eyes. What unintended consequences will our children inherit? Now that alternative styles of marriage are becoming legal, what will be the long term results? When couples choose just to live together, what other kinds of problems are we creating? We are failing to realize we are just perpetuating family problems, not solving them.

## More Challenges

The issues facing our way of life do not end with modernists and postmodernists. A recent article in *USA Today* reported that, "elements of Eastern religions and New Age thinking have been widely adopted by 65% of adults, including many who call themselves Protestants and Catholics according to the Pew Forum on Religion and Public Life."[10]

Practices include astrology, meditation, channeling, crystal healing, astral projection, psychic experiences, holistic health, simple living, whole foods, vegetarianism, as well as an emphasis on environmentalism. Many popular television programs, movies, and talk shows trumpet the ideas of Mother Earth and brother animal on a daily basis. Even some of the cartoons and movies our children watch promote this. Some of us who are older will remember the musical *Hair* that made the Age of Aquarius popular.

Eastern religions, New Age thinking, modernism and post-modernism, and other belief systems continue to impact our way of life. They have created a world that feeds into the human tendency to move toward the lowest, easiest path of resistance. Some find themselves mired in the low way, and others are groping "in between on the misty flats." We ask ourselves, "How did we get here?" All of these man-made belief systems fail at a critical point; they cannot change the human heart.

The failure to account for human sinful tendencies leads us to becoming enablers of human weaknesses. The tragic mistake of justifying ungodly lifestyles leaves in its wake a host of social problems, personal dysfunction and unhappiness. Former Secretary of Education William Bennett concludes that, "We have become the kind of society that civilized countries used to send missionaries to."[11] This has happened slowly, catching most of us unprepared.

It is a battle for our minds. Unless we as believers change the way we think and live we will be engulfed by the surging tide of secular ideas. This is the world in which each of us needs a strong biblical understanding of kingdom principles to show us how to live a God inspired life. We must learn these principles to excel in our world.

[1]Charles Colson and Nancy Pearcey, *How Now Shall We Live?* (Wheaton, IL.: Tyndale, 1999), 22-23.

[2]Bill O'Reilly, *Culture Warrior* (New York: Broadway Books, 2006), 2.

[3]Graham Johnston, *Preaching to a Postmodern World* (Grand Rapids: Baker, 2001), 24-26.

[4]Ibid., 26-59.

[5]Wade Clark Roof, *A Generation of Seekers: The Spiritual Journeys of the Baby Boom Generation* (San Francisco: Harper San Francisco, 1993), 226.

[6]Campbell Brown, "Rev. Franklin Graham on Islam." Posted on December 11, 2009. campbellbrown.blogs.cnn.com. Accessed June 6, 2011.

[7]John Simon, "Art or Child's Play? A Four-Year-Old Could Do It." *Sunday Times Telegraph* (February 14, 1993).

[8]Charles Colson and Nancy Pearcey, *How Now Shall We Live?* (Wheaton, IL.: Tyndale, 1999), 178.

[9]John P. Martin, "Fewer of the Marrying Kind." *The Philadelphia Enquirer* (May 29, 2011), 1.

[10]Catherine L. Grossman, *USA Today*, 12/10/2009.

[11]David Youndt, *Beggaring Belief,* © Scripps Howard News Service. September 4, 2000.

## Further study, reflection, and discussion:

1. What do we know about the core beliefs of the people for whom we voted in the last election?
2. Do we monitor what our children are taught in public school?
3. What current local, state or national issues involve the ideas of the belief systems mentioned in this chapter?
4. What television programs or movies have we have watched recently which expressed these ideas?
5. What popular music to which we listen mentions these ideas in their lyrics?
6. What books have we and our children read that promote these ideas?

# 4

# What's Happening in the Church?

Superficiality is the curse of our age. The doctrine of instant satisfaction is a primary problem. The desperate need for today is not for a greater number of intelligent people, or gifted people, but for deep people. —*Richard Foster*

The battle for our minds takes place on many levels. The demands of where we live and work each day press in on us. These pressures signal our need to learn and apply the principles of living a God inspired life. It is vital that our churches help us win this struggle.

Jerome came home from school one day with a hand-out paper. When his mother asked to see his homework, she discovered the hand-out was a drawing showing the evolution of man from primates. How can Jerome's mother help him to learn a Christian perspective on science?

Matt is a lawyer who works for the state youth and children services. He recently was given a case involving the adoption of a child by two men. How can Matt respond to this case?

Zach and Julie were watching a new program on television when a scene developed showing two women becoming intimate. What guidelines can they use to guide them in their choice of programs and videos?

Cecilia worked as a nurse for an ob/gyn doctor who decided to start offering abortion as a part of his practice. What should Cecilia say to the doctor?

How would we handle these situations as believers? We face a constant stream of serious challenges like this from our culture. How prepared are we to deal with these issues from a Christian point of view? How successful has the church been in preparing us to face the demands of a culture that seeks to mold us with its ideas and lifestyle?

Numerous polls in recent years consistently indicate we are woefully unprepared.[1] There is little statistical difference in the ethics and behavior of Christians and non-believers. Favorable ratings for clergy have declined due to scandals involving sex and the misuse of money. Other polling reveals a significant number who have stopped attending church because of painful, unhappy experiences with a congregation that left them feeling hurt and ignored. We must ask ourselves the question, "Where have we gone wrong in the church?"

# The Battle for Our Minds

It is crucial that we know the dangers of the belief systems that seek to control our way of life. Charles Colson and Nancy Pearcy have aptly described the current state in the church.

> A debilitating issue in modern evangelicalism is that we've been fighting cultural skirmishes on all sides without knowing what the war itself is about. We have not identified the worldviews that lie at the root of cultural conflict – and this ignorance dooms our best efforts.[2]

Unfortunately our churches far too often reflect the impact of this ignorance. Could it be that we are trying to solve surface problems that fail to deal with deeper issues? This is not the picture of moral excellence we need.

As a church we are caught in the cultural crosscurrents of an ever changing modern world. Our day mirrors that of the Bible where the nation of Israel and the church of the first century wrestled with the ungodly influences of their time. The difficulty is the same because the biblical way of life is severely at odds with our culture. As many polls indicate, we are not doing well in this cultural battle.

One of the most pressing problems we face is biblical illiteracy. "The Christian body in America is immersed in a crisis of biblical illiteracy," warns researcher George Barna. "How else can you describe matters when most churchgoing adults reject the accuracy of the Bible, reject the existence of Satan, claim that Jesus sinned, see no need to evangelize, believe that good works are one of the keys to persuading God to forgive their sins, and describe their commitment to Christianity as moderate or even less firm?"[3]

One young person was overheard describing his church youth group as nothing but entertainment. Test scores at Christian colleges reveal a decline in Bible knowledge among entering freshmen. Many Christians have only a superficial knowledge of the Bible and struggle to answer simple questions about what it teaches. Many have to read the Bible to discover that Sodom and Gomorrah were not husband and wife. It is estimated that only one in ten Christians use biblical principles to decide what is right and wrong.

This situation has happened because many of us lack the commitment to read and study the Bible on a regular basis. Sadly many churches are weak in offering opportunities to study the Scriptures. Some small groups offer only socializing opportunities. Some use a random, haphazard assortment of CDs, DVDs and books about Christian topics, while the Bible is hardly opened. Some churches are content to offer only a Sunday morning service characterized by a sermon of feel-good ideas lacking in solid biblical content and theological understanding.

Our biblical illiteracy has led to a predictable lack of commitment to Christian values. Little emphasis is given to studying the Bible, leaving many believers unable to stand against a culture that seeks to impose its godless way of life on everyone. If we are to live a godly life in this kind of world, we must learn how to swim against a strong, swift flowing current of ungodly influences. This is critical not only for us as individuals but also for the survival of the Christian family.

## Contemporary Issues

The church, as it should, has tried to adjust to a changing world by developing strategies to be more contemporary. Changes have been made in many areas, from architecture, to music, to the names used to describe programs and leaders. While some have handled this change well, some things have been hastily cast aside by others.

One pastor was heard on a Sunday morning telling the congregation, "If you don't like it here, I have a list of other churches you can attend." Compassion and sensitivity to those who struggle with the emotions of sudden change have been replaced in some places with a hard line that does nothing more than show people the door despite their many years of faithful service and support.

Ministry to the younger generation is emphasized because they are more likely to accept Christ. We base our methods of reaching the lost on marketing research rather than the fact that Jesus came to die for the sins of the whole world—young, old and in between. The message being sent, especially to those who are older is, "If you don't fit the demographic profile, we are not very interested in you." Unfortunately, some older believers tend to resist change because it moves them out of long established comfort zones. We need to ask ourselves, "What's wrong with this picture?"

Some churches, attempting to be seeker friendly, have also lost the conviction of biblical truth while emphasizing an external atmosphere. Some are reluctant to quote Jesus' words in John 14:6, "I am the way, the truth and the life. No one comes to the Father except through me." After all, we do not want to offend people, they might not return.

The belief in hell is not mentioned for the same reason. Some openly state they do not believe there is a hell. Only God's love is stressed, never His justice and righteousness. Is it any wonder that many Christians suffer from what some have labeled "easy believism" or a belief without moral change or commitment to biblical values?

Media saturates our world with positive and negative results, including the church. Unfortunately, some preachers get their sermons from the internet rather than through personal Bible study. Some churches use a whatever-works approach to attract a crowd to decide what is done on Sunday morning.

The biblical message has become secondary to our methods. In some instances methods even clash with or demean its meaning. The urge to mimic secular entertainment is encouraged because this is what the people want. It's what will draw the people. Have we lost sight of what Jesus called "the narrow gate"?

This approach appeals to those of us who have become entertainment junkies. We are observers who like to see without involvement. We are satisfied with an emotional rush but make no commitment to serve or live by Christian values. Looking around in some churches reveals many who are not involved in worship but are just watching the worship band perform. Have we made the mistake of putting Christian words into secular packages? Do we just copy others rather than using our God given gifts of creativity?

Unfortunately, efforts to create a contemporary atmosphere in some places have created superficial relationships where we lack sufficient opportunities for genuine, meaningful fellowship. Some end up experiencing loneliness in a crowd with a church full of people.

Some churches have a revolving door of visitors, few of whom stay for long. Most people are looking for more than a perfunctory smile and handshake at the door. They are looking for the warmth of inclusion and genuine friendship. We not only need to hear that God is good but how He can help us live a godly life in a world that is unfriendly to our values. Failing to find this, some have opted to stay at home on Sunday and have chosen to go to cyber church by watching a favorite television preacher. Some just play golf, work in the flower garden, or read a good book.

While seeking to change the public image of being legalistic, judgmental, or hypocritical, some churches have allowed the pendulum to swing too far in the other direction. Yielding to the pressures of tolerance and multiculturalism, we have by default become enablers of our modern culture. It appears that in some churches, rather than being counter-culture, we have joined our culture by selectively teaching and preaching those parts of Scripture that do not offend. Our package has become more important than God's message.

## A Warning for Us

Jesus gave a chilling warning concerning the end-time in Matthew 24:10-13,

*At that time many will turn away from the faith and will betray and hate each other, and many false prophets will appear and deceive many*

*people. Because of the increase of wickedness, the love of most will grow cold, but he who stands firm to the end will be saved.*

Warning signs are flashing in contemporary approaches. Is our modern church, even with its contemporary emphasis, still too institutional instead of relational in its emphasis? Are we more concerned with having the right programs and neglect people who do not fit the profile of those programs, namely the older generation? Could it be that the change to a more contemporary approach has missed a more fundamental need to teach us how to live in moral excellence?

If the church is to impact the modern world it will not be done by simply accommodating the ways of the surrounding culture. It can only be done by those who are committed to a sound, biblical way of the life. We must understand the battle that rages with ungodly worldviews for the allegiance of our hearts and minds. We need to learn the biblical principles necessary to win this battle and build God's great kingdom for our day and time.

It is not enough to pack the church building on Sunday morning. The greatest impact of our church is not on Sunday mornings but where each of us lives and works each day of the week. This is where our faith really counts. It is critical for our churches to give believers like Jerome, Matt, Zach, Julie, and Cecilia the knowledge and training they need to live in a secular world seeking to impose its way of life on them. It is vital that we take advantage of opportunities to learn these truths. We cannot excel in our world without it. We must not be left "in between on the misty flats" to "drift to and fro."

[1]See www.barna.org and www.gallop.com.
[2]Charles Colson and Nancy Pearcey, *How Now Shall We Live?* (Wheaton, IL.: Tyndale, 1999), 17.
[3]Barna Research Online, "Religious Beliefs Vary Widely by Denomination," www.barna.org/cgi-bin/PagePressRelease.asp?PressReleaseID=92& Reference=B, June 25, 2001.

## Further study, reflection, or discussion:

1. What challenges did the Jews face in Nehemiah 13 and what are the implications for the church?
2. How can the church be contemporary without compromising biblical truth?
3. How can we help our church offer more opportunities to study the Bible?
4. Why is it important to study the Bible along with CDs and other books?
5. Why is it important to study the Bible with other believers?

# 5

# Fingerprints

*Every tomorrow has two handles. We can take hold of it by the handle of anxiety, or by the handle of faith.* —*Henry Ward Beecher*

It is interesting to see the fervor with which some atheists attack the belief in God by others. They seem to spend a lot of time telling everyone what they are against. The *New York Times* posted this story before Christmas in 2010.

Among the many advertisements lining Interstate 495 in New Jersey en route to the Lincoln Tunnel is a new one promoting atheism for the holidays rather than another gift. The billboard shows three crowned men riding camels toward a humble manger in which a man and woman kneel beside a straw-filled bassinet, all silhouetted beneath a prominent six-pointed star. The message—"You Know It's a Myth: This Season, Celebrate Reason!"—is emblazoned in large white letters above the nativity scene. The provocative 14-by-48-foot billboard was rented for $20,000 by American Atheists, a national atheist organization.[1]

Atheists say they use reason as the basis for not believing in God. Something more seems at work, however. Psalm 14:1 describes those who defy God this way, "The fool has said in his heart, 'There is no God.'"

Belief in God is more than just the exercise of the mind; it is also a matter of our hearts and wills. Denial of God is often used by some as a convenient way to justify certain lifestyles. It puts us in control of our own lives without any objective moral standards. We can make our own rules. But what a sad, empty way to end one's life on earth, believing in nothing but reason and facing nothing.

It is to this world we are called to represent the God who gives our lives meaning, purpose, and the hope of eternal life with Him. He is the one who can give us the foundation to build a life of moral excellence.

## The Fingerprints of God

Whatever the reason, we're told by atheists that we must choose not to believe in God in the face of overwhelming evidence. The Bible does not try to prove God's existence; it just tells us to look at the evidence. It begins with the assumption that God is.

The opening verses of Genesis declare "in the beginning God." Psalm 19:1 states "The heavens declare the glory of God; the skies proclaim the work of his hands." Paul said in Romans 1:20 "Since the creation of the world God's invisible qualities—his eternal power and divine nature—have been clearly seen, being understood from what has been made, so that man is without excuse." The Bible is telling us to look at the world and the heavens.

Like a detective looking for fingerprints, we can look for the fingerprints of God, which are found everywhere. If you see a clock ticking and keeping time, you assume someone made it function that way. The fingerprints of design, order, and complexity are self evident. Yet a clock pales into insignificance when compared to our universe.

The size, order, and complexity of creation speak volumes. The force of gravity in our universe is set at just the right level so that the universe keeps expanding at the proper rate. Too little or too much and our universe would not exist today. The same fine tuning is found in the atom where the size and electrical charges of electrons and protons are precisely set. Physical properties and the position of the earth in orbit around the sun are also finely tuned. Why are these settings important? Without this precision, human life could not exist.

The human body is another example of the fingerprints of God. DNA is a complex means of chemical communication found in living organisms. It is compared to an extremely complex computer program. It's like a blueprint used to determine how each of us develops. Scientists have discovered recently that our circadian rhythm of sleep and waking is determined by our blood chemistry.

The human eye also is a marvel of complexity and precision. We have not one but two of them. It is amazing that what our eyes see is upside down but our brains turn it right side up, all without conscious thought. It's an astonishing fact. It takes a lot of faith to believe these things were brought into being by natural forces and random chance.

How does the atheist explain the purpose of the concept of love, the enjoyment of beauty, and all the intangibles of life that give us pleasure? They would tell us these things are simply electro-chemical impulses in our brains that are the result of the mindless forces of nature. Is that all there is to the toothless smile and cooing of a baby? What is it that warms our heart, brings smiles to our faces, and causes us to babble to them?

It is the atheist who chooses to close his mind to the evidence. Some people readily accept the theories of quantum physics about parallel, multidimensional universes. Even though they cannot see these universes nor verify them by scientific experiment, it is considered serious scientific investigation because they are looking for evidence and clues. Yet they refuse to recognize the evidence and clues of God's fingerprints in His creation.

Some, called deists, suggest that God did create the universe like a giant clock. He has wound it up and left it to run by the set laws of nature. They believe that there is no supernatural intervention in the affairs of humans who inhabit a tiny speck in a vast cosmos.

When you think about it, this is really no different from the world of the atheist. God is not a part of either of their worlds. He is not there for the atheist, and He is far away for the deist. We are alone with no direction, no help, and nothing in which to hope except ourselves. The tragedy is that we continue trying to lift ourselves from intractable problems by our bootstraps, only to find there are no bootstraps.

The Bible does not teach this concept about God, however. Colossians 1:15-20 states concerning Christ,

> *He is the image of the invisible God, the firstborn over all creation. For by him all things were created: things in heaven and on earth, visible and invisible, whether thrones or powers or rulers or authorities; all things were created by him and for him. He is before all things, and in him all things hold together. And he is the head of the body, the church; he is the beginning and the firstborn from among the dead, so that in everything he might have the supremacy. For God was pleased to have all his fullness dwell in him, and through him to reconcile all things, whether things on earth or things in heaven, making peace through his blood, shed on the cross.*

God in Christ is supremely involved in this world to reconcile all things to Himself. Hebrews 1:3 declares that Christ is "sustaining all things by his powerful word." Without Christ, there would be no chance of reconciliation with God, and our world would cease to exist if His sustaining power were removed.

## The Power of Our Lives

As believers, though, we must understand the atheist and the deist will not be drawn to God by our ability to reason. The door to a person's heart and will must be opened from the inside. They may not want to listen to what we say, but they can see the fingerprints of God in our lives. Like the rest of creation we can live lives that are pointing to God. The development of godly character and the quality of our lives will be powerful evidence that cannot be easily ignored. God's love and goodness can shine through our words and actions where we live and work each day.

While often used as an excuse to avoid God, one of the greatest hindrances people cite is the time-worn accusation that Christians are hypocrites. We can live in such a way that they will be challenged to change their opinions. We can be God's fingerprints to a broken world that refuses to recognize Him or give Him glory for the majesty and beauty of what He has created. The quality of our lives really can make a difference when we share about God.

Our changed lives are powerful influences in speaking to a lost world. People who do not believe in God will argue the fine points of science and philosophy, but when they are faced with a person whose life exhibits the love and grace of God there is not much they can criticize. The story of Kim Phuc is told by Charles Colson and Nancy Pearcey.

Those of us who are older will remember the photo of Kim that appeared in newspapers across the country in 1972. She was the little girl running naked down a Vietnamese road. Her clothes had been burned away. Her skin was blackened by the burns from napalm dropped by a United States pilot. She almost died but lived and endured seventeen surgeries.

What many people do not know about Kim is that she was converted to the Christian faith by a brother-in-law who was a strong Christian. Kim eventually married; something she thought would never happen because of her burned, disfigured body. Returning from their honeymoon in Moscow, the plane stopped in Newfoundland, Canada. She and her new husband made a quick decision to defect, leaving all their worldly possessions on board the plane.

Kim was invited in 1996 to speak at the Veterans Day ceremonies held at the Vietnam War Memorial in Washington, D. C. During her brief speech she mentioned, "Even if I could talk face-to-face with the pilot who dropped the bomb, I could tell him we cannot change history, but we should try to do good things for the present and for the future to promote peace."

After receiving a thunderous applause, she received a note from a policeman. It read, "I'm the man you are looking for." She agreed to meet with him. When they met she hugged the man and he began to sob, saying, "I am sorry. I am just so sorry." Kim replied, "It is okay. I forgive. I forgive." Her favorite Bible verse is from Luke 6:37, "Forgive, and you will be forgiven."[2] How do you explain away a life of moral excellence like this?

Many people want to know what God is like. They do not know because of the fog of ignorance and the many voices claiming to speak for or against Him. What they can see is our lives. Most of us will not have dramatic stories like Kim Phuc. Her story came as a result of immense pain and suffering, something we will hopefully never experience.

We all have a story, however. People around us can read our daily lives. They can see God's fingerprints on us. We have a positive message of faith, hope and love that is worth embracing. Let us live in such a way that the non-believer can say, "I want what you have."

John 3:16 gives us a picture of what God is like. It says,

*For God so loved the world that he gave his one and only Son, that whoever believes in him shall not perish but have eternal life.*

God is not somewhere far away. Rather, His love and righteousness have met in the atoning work of Christ to give us the promise of eternal life.

While God is not seen nor studied through scientific experiments, yet we look at His fingerprints in the world and affirm in our hearts that He is the Creator. Our faith declares, "God has revealed Himself to me in Christ Jesus." As we yield ourselves to God, He will put His fingerprints on our hearts and lives. It's how we can represent Him to a skeptical world. It's the kind of excellence our world needs to see.

[1]Daniel Slotnik, cityroom.blogs.nytimes.com/2010/11/29/for the holidays an atheism billboard. Accessed November 12, 2011.
[2]Charles Colson and Nancy Pearcey, *How Now Shall We Live?* (Wheaton, IL.: Tyndale, 1999), 480-486.

## Further study, reflection, and discussion:

1. Study Psalm 19:1-6 and meditate on its message.
2. What attitudes are expressed about God and the world of creation in Job 38-39; Psalm 8; Psalm 29 and Psalm 104?
3. What does the atheist use for guidance in his/her life?
4. What does the believer use for guidance in his/her life?

6

# The King and His Reign

*If I find in myself a desire which no experience can satisfy, the most probable explanation is that I was made for another world.* —*C.S. Lewis*

Prince William, the future king of England, and Kate Middleton captured the imagination of the world when they were married at Westminster Abbey on April 29, 2011. Millions, some say even billions, watched with rapt attention. The color and the pageantry, along with a beautiful bride and a handsome prince, seemed like a fairy tale out of a book. Now the prince and his wife travel the world to the delight of people everywhere.

But many in our country, though they find royalty intriguing, would not like to live under a monarchy. Everything about kings and kingdoms seems so fanciful and distant. We live in a democracy where liberty and the freedom of personal choices were won in a difficult and risky rebellion against the rule of a powerful monarch, King George III, and the mighty British Empire.

## Two Kingdoms

When we read in the Bible about Jesus' reference to the kingdom of God, many have a difficult time relating to this idea. Today, postmodernists tell us to be suspicious of all authority. Why should we give up our freedoms to live under the outdated idea of a king and his desire to reign over us?

Since this is exactly what Jesus calls us to do, let's explore what this means to us as believers. As we learn more of what the Bible teaches, we will learn there are two kingdoms, one ruled by God and one ruled by Satan.

J. R. R. Tolkien's trilogy, *The Lord of the Rings,* captures this theme. It is a classic tale of the clash between good and evil. The Dark Lord Saurin plots to take the ring that would give him the power to rule over all. The story pulsates with drama as Frodo Baggins and his companions travel to Mordor to destroy the ring at Mount Doom.

Paul described our struggle with Satan's kingdom in Ephesians 6:12, "For our struggle is not against flesh and blood, but against the rulers, against the au-thorities, against the powers of this dark world and against the spiritual forces of evil in the heavenly realms." As believers, we live in dynamic tension between these two kingdoms. The many decisions we make each day determine whether we are living by the principles of God's kingdom or Satan's kingdom.

As we consider the kingdom of God, three things need to be determined: the ruler or king, the place or people where the king rules, and the rules or principles the king uses to govern his kingdom. Jesus used these ideas to teach who He was and how He wants us to live.

## The King

The Jews of the time of Christ looked for the coming of the Messiah or the Anointed One. They interpreted various Old Testament passages indicating the Messiah King would come and restore the kingdom of David to Israel by defeating their enemies. They hoped the Messiah would lead a mighty army to drive the hated Roman oppressors from the land of Israel. They emphasized the Victorious King of Psalm 110 but failed to realize the Suffering Servant of Isaiah 53 had to come first.

Even Jesus' disciples after the resurrection asked Him in Acts 1:6, "Lord, are you at this time going to restore the kingdom to Israel?" Jesus obviously did not meet these expectations. His disciples failed at first to understand the real truth of what God accomplished in Christ. Jesus was the Messiah King, but He would be quite different from that of a military deliverer. He did not come to conquer with a sword but through a cross.

Jesus' death on the cross was necessary before His reign as King over the hearts and lives of His followers. Without Jesus' death to redeem mankind, there would be no people in His kingdom. It was only later His disciples came to realize the greater scope of Jesus and His kingdom. It was not to be limited in time nor to the nation of Israel but would span all history and the entire world.

When Prince William becomes king, his role will be mostly ceremonial and a reflection of England's storied past. Jesus, on the other hand, declared in John 18:36, "My kingdom is not of this world." His kingdom would be different from an earthly one. He rejected a political solution to the problems of a fallen world. He chose a redemptive approach where we could be changed from the inside out.

## The Place

Jesus stated in Luke 17:21, "The Kingdom of God is within you." Jesus does not rule from some throne in a faraway place. He wants to come into our hearts and lives and be our King. Some of us may resist this idea since we want to rule and run our own lives. This is what the secular humanists tell us to do. It is what our human nature wants. But what happens when we run out of ideas and life gets too much for us? How do we fix our lives when things go wrong? Where do we turn? How can we avoid making the mistakes that get us into problems that at times seem impossible to solve?

Jesus does not want to make us into spiritual robots. He does not come into our hearts just to spoil our fun. He wants to come into our lives because He knows we are plagued by the problems of sin. He wants to show us how to live so we can avoid the pitfalls of doing things our own way. Jesus comes to help us fix our lives and make them much, much better than we can by ourselves.

Nutritionists tell us oatmeal is good for us to eat. By itself, it's too bland for me. A little pinch of salt, a packet of sweetener along with some butter and milk makes it taste a lot better. I'm not much of a cook, but I've learned to take my spoon and mix the ingredients well into the oatmeal. It tastes much better that way. Jesus does not want to be a convenient add-on to our lives. When we invite Him into our hearts to be our King, He begins to work in every area of our lives. Just like adding and mixing ingredients into oatmeal, it works much better that way.

## The Rules

Our current culture tells us to be skeptical of all authority. We can make our own rules. But how does that work? Does that mean we can get in our sporty cars and drive as fast as we want whenever we want? Does that mean we can eat whatever we want? Can we walk around in public without clothes? Can we just show up for work whenever we choose?

The absurdity speaks for itself. Rules in life are necessary for our own good and the welfare of those around us. This is why Jesus gave us rules or principles. Like a sports car driven too fast, His rules help keep us from crashing because our lives have gotten out of control.

Much of Jesus' teaching focused on the kingdom of God; what it was like, the rules or principles that defined it, and how His followers should live. Matthew 4:23 describes Jesus going "throughout Galilee…preaching the good news of the kingdom."

The Sermon on the Mount in Matthew 5-7 offers a good look into the teachings of Jesus. Set against a backdrop of the Pharisees and teachers of the Law, Jesus corrected many of the misunderstandings of the Old Testament popular in His day. His teachings will help us correct the ideas we have learned from a secular culture.

As was mentioned in the introduction, Jesus' model prayer in Matthew 6:10

teaches us to pray, "Your kingdom come, your will be done on earth as it is in heaven." Many of Jesus' parables illustrate God's kingdom and the principles that govern it. A typical example is found in Matthew 13:44 where Jesus used His favorite introduction to many of His parables, "The kingdom of heaven is like..." He used this theme to help us discover what the kingdom is like and how we should live in it.

As we internalize the principles of His kingdom, we will lay the foundation to excel in our world as believers. We will see in later chapters that the secret is found in the attitude with which we follow our King. We will also discover the foundational principles Jesus taught that are to guide our lives.

## The Future of the Kingdom

This life is not the end of the story. God's kingdom has a future cast to it as well. The Scriptures indicate His kingdom will one day take on visible reality. All that happens in this life is moving toward that glorious day. Paul described it this way in 1 Corinthians 15:24-27,

> *Then the end will come, when he (Jesus) hands over the kingdom to God the Father after he has destroyed all dominion, authority and power. For he must reign until he has put all enemies under his feet. The last enemy to be destroyed is death. For he has put everything under his feet.*

While we live in a democracy that rightly values freedom, it is a flawed, human system. As believers, we look forward to the day when Christ will return and establish His kingdom on the earth. It is then that the enemies of God, led by Satan, will be destroyed like the ring in Tolkien's book. Christ's rule will be absolute and complete.

In the meantime, let us choose to follow our King and thoroughly mix His kingdom principles into our lives here and now. This will help us keep our lives under control and avoid the pitfalls of sinful living. It is how we can begin to excel in our world as people who have chosen to follow Christ.

## Further study, reflection, and discussion:

1. Use the Scriptures in this chapter for more detailed personal or group study.
2. What can we learn about God's kingdom from the Parable of the Sower in Matthew 13:1-9, 18-23?
3. What comparison did Paul make in Ephesians 2:1-10?
4. What did Paul encourage believers to do in Ephesians 6:10-20?
5. What do we learn from Revelation 11:15?

7

# Where Are We Headed?

*God gives us dreams a size too big so that we can grow in them.*
— *Author Unknown*

The problem with exercising on treadmills is it can get awfully boring going nowhere. Something is needed to change the routine and break the monotony. Many people listen to music, watch television, or even read a book. Some of us may feel like we are on a treadmill, walking without direction, meandering through life. The routines of raising children, going to work, and seeking a few momentary pleasures in life have become boring and unfulfilling. We seem to be just waiting for tomorrow. A satisfying and fulfilling life seems like an ever receding horizon. We sense something is missing, but we are not sure what it is.

There are many people like this, caught "in between on the misty flats." They "drift to and fro" missing a fuller, richer, and more meaningful life. Our lack of purpose in life is because of a basic problem called sin. It obscures our view and clouds our understanding so that we fail to see God's purposes for our lives. As a result, we settle for substitutes which fail to satisfy, leaving that underlying sense of something missing.

Rick Warren succinctly stated, "God has not left us in the dark to wonder and guess."[1] God's remedy for this is found in what He has done for us by sending His Son, Jesus. Once His kingdom comes into our hearts, our lives take on direction and meaning. Life need never be boring again.

## Headed for Glory

My wife and I were able to visit the Sistine Chapel at the Vatican on a recent trip to Italy. We stood in awe in the Vatican art galleries, marveling at the profusion of artistic creations. It was sensory overload. The intricate detail on a grand scale spoke of the skill and talent of Michelangelo and many other artists.

The magnificence of their creations reminded us of all God has done in Christ. It is like a masterpiece of art, declaring the glory and majesty of God's skill and accomplishments in our salvation. Each of us is like a vast unfolding canvas, displaying God's redemption in His Son and speaking to the world about the glory of His mercy, grace, and love. Paul describes this succinctly in Ephesians 1:3-14. Verse 1 summarizes it well, "Praise be to the God and Father of our Lord Jesus Christ, who has blessed us in the heavenly realms with every spiritual blessing in Christ."

However, we are not just two-dimensional characters in a painting or fresco. God wants us to be three-dimensional people who bring glory to Him in the everyday world of real life. Paul explained this in 1 Corinthians 10:31 where he wrote, "So whether you eat or drink, or whatever you do, do it all for the glory of God." The immediate context deals with eating food offered to idols, but Paul gives the broader principle by stating, "whatever you do."

Our daily purpose is to bring glory to God in all we do. Our daily lives do not need to be an endless cycle of meaningless tasks on life's treadmill. As we follow Christ, everything we do has meaning and purpose because it can bring glory to God. Nothing is trivial or unimportant in His kingdom.

Take this one step further. It is not just a one-way street. God not only wants us to glorify Him in all we do, but He also wants us to share in His glory. Second Corinthians 3:18 tells us, "And we, who with unveiled faces all reflect the Lord's glory, are being transformed into his likeness with ever-increasing glory." Think about it. God has begun a process in us designed to change us to reflect His glory more and more. The results of sin have left us like mirrors that have lost the shiny reflective coating. God is restoring that coating so we can reflect Him more clearly.

God said in Genesis 1:26, "Let us make man in our image and in our likeness." God is in the process of restoring the glory of who He is in our lives. He will do it every day in the ordinary events of life and it will not be boring. One day God's process of restoring His image in our lives will be complete. Paul exclaimed in 1 Corinthians 15:42-44, "So will it be with the resurrection of the dead. The body that is sown perishable, it is raised imperishable; it is sown in dishonor, it is raised in glory; it is sown in weakness, it is raised in power; it is sown a natural body, it is raised a spiritual body." What a glorious future, to stand in the presence of God and His glory sharing the wonder of all He is! We are important to God. All we do each day can have a place in God's great masterpiece of redemption as we reflect His glory. There is more to the story, however.

## Chosen for Holiness

As a kid growing up, from time to time Joey went through the agony of being chosen for a team whether it was on the playground or some in-class activity. Joey was not a good athlete. He also was a slow learner. As a result he was always chosen last. It was embarrassing and humiliating to stand at the end of the line. He knew in his heart even then that he was not really wanted.

One day a friend decided to stand up for Joey and chose him first. His friend was a Christian and felt compelled to take Joey's side despite his weaknesses. There are many Joeys in our world. Whether we have suffered like Joey or not, all of us have a deeply felt need to be wanted, to be chosen and to have value. Ephesians 1:11 tells us "In him we were also chosen." Like Joey's friend, our friend is Jesus. He has taken our side. As believers and members of God's kingdom, He has called and chosen us with a specific goal in mind. This goal explains the process of how we can glorify God. There is good news for all of us. We are not left-over, marginal choices with Him. Each of us is important in His Kingdom.

First Peter 1:13-16 gives us specific insight into what this goal involves. It states,

*Therefore, prepare your minds for action; be self-controlled; set your hope fully on the grace given you when Jesus Christ is revealed. As obedient children, do not conform to the evil desires you had when you lived in ignorance. But just as he who called you is holy, so be holy in all you do; for it is written, "Be holy, because I am holy."*

We are to get ready for what God wants to do. He has chosen to set us on a path to holiness. That might seem like a scary and unreachable goal. Before bailing out, however, let's take some time to explore what this means.

First of all, it is important to realize that holiness is not something we have to produce on our own. 2 Corinthians 5:21 teaches us, "God made him (Jesus) who had no sin to be sin for us, so that in him we might become the righteousness of God." Since we are sinners and incapable of becoming holy by our own efforts, God used the work of Jesus on the cross to lay the foundation for righteousness and holiness in our lives. When we accept Christ into our hearts and enter His kingdom, He becomes the righteousness we cannot produce for ourselves.

Experiencing God's love and forgiveness in Christ is wonderful, but He does not want us to remain spiritual infants. We are to be actively involved in God's kingdom, not sitting on the sidelines. When we play a sport, none of us likes to be a bench warmer. Paul put it this way in Philippians 2:12-13, "Continue to work out your salvation with fear and trembling, for it is God who works in you to will and to act according to his good purpose." God calls each of us to be His special people and to reflect His holy character. As God actively works to accomplish this, He wants our cooperation and effort to live practical holy lives.

Romans 8:29 provides more detail telling us we are "to be conformed to the likeness of his Son." Think of it. We are ultimately to be like Jesus. First John 3:2 gives a glimpse into this, "Dear friends, now we are children of God, and what we will be has not yet been made known. But we know that when he appears, we shall be like him, for we shall see him as he is." There is nothing second rate about God's plans for us. As we cooperate with Him, our lives are given a clear sense of direction. Even the negative things that touch us can be used to shape and form us because of this wonderful goal.

When we think of holy people we are apt to envision someone who lives like a recluse, removed from the real world. Some lived in caves or remote places to escape the world around them. Many years ago one man, Simeon Stylites, lived atop a pole for thirty-six years. People like this are often depicted today in stories and the media as living simple lives of poverty and self denial. They are definitely different from the rest of us. This is not what the Bible teaches, however. The biblical concept is actually one of separation from sin and dedication to God.

While holiness will have an effect on our outward appearance, its basic emphasis is on our inward natures—how we think and act toward God and others. If we get our hearts and minds in the right place, our outer appearance will follow. We do not have to look like the media caricatures either.

## Hungry To Be Holy

Babies are a delight to watch. It is fascinating to watch a hungry new born baby gulp formula from a bottle. A baby does not have to be taught to do this. They come preprogrammed.

First Peter 2:1-3 used this metaphor to challenge us,

*Therefore, rid yourselves of all malice and all deceit, hypocrisy, envy and slander of every kind. Like newborn babies, crave pure spiritual milk, so that by it you may grow up in your salvation, now that you have tasted that the Lord is good.*

Putting aside the old way of sinful living, coupled with a hunger and desire for spiritual things, is needed for growth toward holiness.

Babies like to eat regularly and often. They end up smearing food all over their faces while the milk dribbles down their chins. That's because they're hungry. So how hungry are we? Simply put, as believers, we will want to take advantage of regular and systematic opportunities to grow in the Lord. The importance of personal Bible reading and prayer along with church organized times for study and fellowship have already been noted.

When Jesus chose His disciples He recruited ordinary people like you and me. He used these men to change the world. Based on these things, God wants us to use what He is developing in us to be a witness to an unbelieving world. We can have a powerful and positive effect on the world around us rather than passively absorbing our sinful culture.

Unlike the Israelites in the Old Testament who rejected God and pursued the gods of their day, we can pursue God's call to holiness in our lives. While millions of people spend their lives pursuing the emptiness of the good life, we can concentrate on becoming like Jesus and develop an inner beauty that will never fade. Paul boldly declared in Philippians 3:12, "Not that I have already obtained this, or have already been made perfect, but I press on to take hold of that for which Christ Jesus took hold of me."

Where are we headed? We can get off the treadmill and begin glorifying God. We can glorify God by seeking to become holy like His Son, Jesus. It can happen every day in the ordinary events of our lives.

As we seek to glorify God, our lives will increasingly shine with the brilliance of His glory and the purity of the holiness of Jesus. One day this process will be completed. We will be like our Lord Jesus. The Sistine Chapel and the Vatican art galleries will pale in comparison. In the meantime, we can hunger like a baby for spiritual food. We can be like Paul, stretching out like a runner in a race toward the finish line. It is how we are meant to excel for God in our world.

[1]Rick Warren, *The Purpose Driven Life* (Grand Rapids, MI.: Zondervan, 2002), 20.

## Further study, reflection, and discussion:

1. Use the Scriptures in this chapter for more detailed personal or group study.
2. What has been the driving sense of purpose in our lives?
3. Why is it important to think of ourselves as a masterpiece God is creating?
4. Why is it important to see God at work in the small, ordinary things in our daily lives?
5. What does 1 Corinthians 15:35-58 teach us we can expect after we die?
6. Why does the idea of holiness seem frightening and unrealistic?
7. How does it make us feel to know that God has chosen us to be like His Son?
8. What changes can we make in our lives to develop a godlier life style?

8

# Are Two Better Than One?

*But if serving the Lord seems undesirable to you, then choose for your-*
*selves this day whom you will serve* (Joshua 24:15a).

Two-headed turtles have been found from time to time in different places.
As expected, people are always fascinated with them. One of the interesting
things about the turtle is to see the tug-of-war between the two heads over a
piece of meat it is fed. Meal time becomes a battle. Having two heads does not
work out so well for the turtles.

Many times we are like these turtles, drawn in different directions over con-
flicting decisions. What are our choices each day? Do we take the easy road of
indulgence or the harder path of self-control? What attitudes form the foundation we use to view life and others? How do we view ourselves? These are
questions we tend to avoid because taking a hard look at ourselves can be
painful.

But if we are going to glorify God by becoming holy, it will be necessary to
take a look at the thoughts and attitudes that motivate our behavior. We will
have to choose a different path from the one learned from our sinful nature and
secular culture. We cannot serve God and something else at the same time. Two
are not better than one when it comes to moral excellence.

Jesus gave us specific insight into this different path in the Beatitudes in
Matthew 5:3-10. The starting point for a different path begins with the first
Beatitude, "Blessed are the poor in spirit, for theirs is the kingdom of heaven."
He said the path to happiness (the meaning of blessed) begins with being poor
in spirit. Jesus said that recognizing our sinfulness or spiritual poverty is what
allows us into the kingdom of heaven where true and lasting happiness is to be
found. This is what leads us to find our true value and self worth through God's
redeeming work in Christ.

This seems like a contradiction since we have been told to emphasize the
power of positive thinking. We have been taught that man is basically good. We
are not supposed to think negative thoughts, otherwise we cannot be happy.
That's why Jesus' teaching is such a different path.

One of the major stumbling blocks to godly living is our pride. How many
times have we heard someone who has committed a crime say, "I'm not really a

bad person." Most of us have not committed a crime, but Romans 3:23 is clear, "All have sinned and fallen short of the glory of God."

Some of us can swim fifty yards. Some can even swim five miles, but none of us can swim to Bermuda or Hawaii. The truth is when we measure ourselves with others, we can look good, but when compared with God's glory, none of us makes the grade. It is the recognition of this fact that opens the gate to a different path.

Jesus continues in the second Beatitude by stating another seeming contradiction, "Blessed are those who mourn, for they will be comforted." How can this be? Back in 1988 Bobby McFerrin's song "Don't Worry, Be Happy" reached number one on the Billboard Hot 100 chart.[1] Everyone wants to be happy. But people who exercise have a saying, "no pain; no gain." Jesus is teaching us the path to happiness begins, not with laughter and fun, but with a genuine sorrow for our sinfulness. Denial or being blasé about the sin in our lives does not solve the problem. We are only hiding it from ourselves.

We cannot solve the dysfunction of sin in our lives by knowledge alone. Recognizing our sin, coupled with a genuine sorrow for it, is the cure that leads to the path of true happiness. Only this can lead to the comfort of God's all redeeming grace and forgiveness in and through Christ Jesus.

He went on to say in the third Beatitude, "Blessed are the meek, for they will inherit the earth." Again, this is the opposite of what our culture teaches. Happiness is associated with winning and being successful. It is a dog-eat-dog world out there. Many people fight, bite, scratch, and lie to gain what they want and then defend it with all vigor and tenacity. The sad thing about this approach is the empty feeling it leaves inside along with destroyed relationships.

While we may suffer material loss at times when living by Jesus' teachings, the gain of a life lived well provides an eternal reward. The life lived in integrity brings the knowledge that we have treated others with respect and dignity. And the knowledge that God is our provider brings a peace and satisfaction that is found in no other way. The way to inherit the earth is not to grasp at the things of this life with greed and selfishness, trying to conquer it at the expense of others. The way to inherit the earth is to live a God inspired life, trusting in Him as the provider of all we really need.

Jesus taught us in the fourth Beatitude, "Blessed are those who hunger and thirst for righteousness, for they will be filled." Have you ever noticed how many things in the store always seem to be marked as new and improved? Our lives will surely be better if we buy it. Then several months later, we see a new package with the same words—new and improved. How quickly our possessions become old and outdated. We live in a materialistic world that cares little for what is good and righteous. Happiness is identified with acquiring the next possession.

Jesus warned us in Matthew 7:21, "For where your treasure is, there your heart will be also." Jesus calls us to focus on what we are to become on the inside instead of pursuing the so-called good life. What truly satisfies is a life spent pursuing God and His righteousness. This is the quest for moral excellence. This is a different path, but one that is deeply satisfying and rewarding.

Jesus continued in the fifth Beatitude showing us the importance of relationships by stating, "Blessed are the merciful, for they will be shown mercy." When someone offends us we often react by wanting to strike back and get even. It is a human reaction. Sometimes we even give in to the urge, especially if we have a short fuse. The momentary satisfaction of getting even, however, leaves us with a hollow feeling deep inside.

How quick are we to be judgmental toward the failings of others? An honest look at ourselves will reveal our own list of shortcomings. We all would like others to be tolerant and forgiving of us when we fail. Jesus is saying what goes around comes around. He explained this further in the Golden Rule in Matthew 7:12, "In everything, do unto others what you would have them do to you."

Jesus continued to probe the inner self in the sixth Beatitude saying, "Blessed are the pure in heart, for they will see God." Many people think happiness is found by throwing off the old fashioned restrictions that bind and narrow their lives. Postmodernists tell us to peel off the layers of the onion and explore all the options that life offers. The problem with this is that selfish and even destructive lifestyles are chosen while consequences are not even considered.

Some of us Christians try to have it both ways by living a secular lifestyle. When we do this, our divided loyalties end up giving us a deep-seated sense of guilt and anxiety. It is not a path to happiness or excellence.

The word *pure* has the meaning of being free from contamination like gold or silver. A trip to the jewelry store tells us the value goes up with the purity. True happiness comes when we examine our lives for those attitudes and actions that offend God, stain our lives, and negatively impact others. Pursuit of a godly way of life brings a sense of cleanness, purity, and peace that will lead us into the presence of God.

Jesus also taught us in the seventh Beatitude, "Blessed are the peacemakers, for they will be called the sons of God." The Scottish poet Robert Burns said it well, "O would some power, the gift to give us, to see ourselves as others see us."

When other people are around us, what do they find? Are we a prickly porcupine or a soft furry kitten? We all know which one not to touch. No one likes to walk near a thorn bush. Even roses are best admired from a distance or carefully picked. Jesus is calling us to be peacemakers not trouble makers. If we are to travel a different path some thorns will need to be removed from our personalities.

Jesus gave us a way to measure our level of commitment to Him in the final Beatitude saying, "Blessed are those who are persecuted because of righteousness, for theirs is the kingdom of heaven." A boat ride down the Colorado River in the Grand Canyon is fun until the rapids are reached. Some people would love to get out and walk at that point. Some actually do. Being a follower of Jesus is easy when times are good, but what is the tipping point for us to turn away from Him and compromise His values? How resolute will we be in the face of adversity? This is a heavy question that takes us to the bedrock of what is important in our lives—serving God or something else.

Few of us will have a gun put to our heads to make this decision, but we are faced each day with decisions about which path to follow. Jesus lets us know our journey to His kingdom is not just a picnic or stroll in the park but is serious business with eternal consequences. The path that leads to moral excellence will not always be easy, but it will be well worth the ride, even a bumpy one.

Jesus gives us a clear choice in the Beatitudes about the path leading to true and lasting happiness. His teachings contradicted those of His day and they stand in stark contrast with our culture today as well. They are like road signs for us showing the road or path to take.

Our sinful nature pulls us toward a secular world. Jesus beckons us to follow Him. Two heads only cause confusion over which path to take. Like the turtles, which head will win? Following Jesus' way requires singleness of purpose. Which path will we choose as we live in our world? Only one leads to excellence in our world.

[1]wikipedia.org/wiki/Don%27t_Worry,_Be_Happy. Accessed July 12, 2011.

## Further study, reflection, and discussion:

1. Compare the Beatitudes in Matthew 5:3-10 with Luke 6:20-26.
2. What does it take to make us happy?
3. Do we view ourselves as good persons? Why? Why not?
4. Do we compare ourselves with others? Why? Why not?
5. How would we describe the path of our lives?
6. Would we describe our personality as a porcupine, a kitten or something else?
7. What is our level of commitment to Christian values?

9

# The Most Excellent Way

*And now I will show you the most excellent way* (1 Corinthians 12:31b).

Patrick and Leena are both new believers who attend Community Fellowship Church. Patrick comes from a home where he was allowed to make his own choices. His parents are progressives who believed their children should decide their own values. Leena comes from a strict Muslim home where she has had to live by her parents beliefs. As their mentors, what should we say to them about following Christ and establishing new Christian values for their lives?

People in our culture today seem to be in a never-ending search for options in their self-determined morality. Their search is characterized by anxiety and a lack of certainty. Their lives are never stable. It is one of the unforeseen consequences of everyone having their own truth. It is what happens when people reject God and His principles for living.

Modern Western culture is in decline. Just as in the time of ancient Israel, our world will reap the results of its own free choices. What about those of us who are believers, followers of Christ? What can we use to build a solid foundation for our lives that does not change with the shifting moods of our current culture? How can we glorify God, become holy like Jesus, and walk the different path?

There are so many different churches, Christian books, and media programs providing a virtual smorgasbord of information for believers. You can Google any Christian topic and get thousands of responses. While it is good that Christians are trying to impact the world using the Internet and other media, the sheer volume of information can be confusing and intimidating.

## The Best Source

What is the most excellent way? Where do we start? Who is right or wrong? How do we sort out all the ideas about living a God-inspired life? It all can seem so complicated and even contradictory at times. But believers can cut through this mountain of information and the opinions of others by starting with the Bible and listening to the words of Jesus Himself. What He taught will simplify and clarify His kingdom principles for us. This is what Patrick and Leena need to hear as they start their journey with Jesus.

Jesus was asked a question by the Pharisees in Matthew 22:36-40, "Teacher, which is the greatest commandment?" Their immediate purpose was to trick Jesus into making a statement they could use to discredit Him. Unwittingly, they opened the door for Jesus to make a profound statement about the basis for all kingdom principles by telling us what the greatest commandment is.

Jesus' answer took the Pharisees back to the very Law they so cherished but misinterpreted. Quoting from Deuteronomy 6:5 in verses 37-38, "Jesus replied, 'Love the Lord your God with all your heart and with all your soul and with all your mind.' This is the first and greatest commandment." He then continues to quote from Leviticus 19:18 in verse 39 saying, "And the second is like it: 'Love your neighbor as yourself.'" He concludes His answer in verse 40 stating, "All the Law and the Prophets hang on these two commandments."

Jesus' answer summarized the basic intent of all the Old Testament's teachings on how God wanted His people to live. He returned the principle of godly living from the legalism of the Pharisees to its original basis of love of God and neighbor. The words "with all your heart and with all your soul and with all your mind" replaced the coercive "have to" of legalism with the "want to" of love.

Jesus revealed that the moral underpinning of the old covenant did not change as He established the new covenant by His death, resurrection, and ascension to heaven. He taught the moral basis of God's kingdom was really a matter of our hearts and our relationships, not just a list of legal do's and don'ts. He reminds us we are not called to live by a long punch list that is soon outdated. The path to moral excellence goes much deeper than that. We are called to express in our lives the very nature of God Himself, "because God is love" (1 John 4:16). Remember, God's goal for us is to become like His Son, Jesus.

## Defining the Issues and Options

Some definitions would be helpful before continuing.[1] Values are those social principles, goals, or standards held or accepted by an individual or a group of people. We attach more or less importance to certain standards than others. Values determine how we make decisions and interact with God and others.

Legalism is using a set of rules to determine how we should live. Moses had given Israel 613 separate laws. There were thousands of interpretations of these laws by Jesus' day, some written and some oral. Different schools of thought had developed over how these laws should be interpreted, making it exceedingly complex and difficult to follow. It was this overlay of interpretations that Jesus set out to correct in the Sermon on the Mount as well as elsewhere in the Gospels.

The Pharisees had obscured the original intent of Moses' Law with their legalistic approach. Some Christian groups in church history as well as today have fallen into the same trap as the Pharisees. They make rules the basis of salvation and develop lists to tell people how to live the Christian life. As a Muslim, Leena grew up in a strict, legalist home so she would have understood this pattern.

Licentiousness, a word not often heard, is the opposite of legalism and is similar in meaning to words like decadence and hedonism. It is descriptive of a lifestyle that is morally unrestrained and lacking in good standards. Many movies and videos today give graphic illustrations of this idea. Giving oneself the license to live and act as one pleases was found throughout the world of the Bible and is still very much a part of our culture today. As we have seen, postmodernism promotes this idea of self-determined morality. This was the atmosphere of Patrick's childhood.

Legalism and licentiousness are too seriously flawed to use for a stable, secure set of values. Legalism collapses under the weight of a long and increasingly complex system of rigid, onerous rules. Licentiousness is ultimately self-destructive. Scandals among public figures document this sad reality on a regular basis.

But Jesus' teaching about love supplies the balance needed between the extremes of legalism and licentiousness. Love, properly understood, provides the only solid foundation on which we can build our lives.

## Clarifying Love

Knowing the basic kingdom principle of love of God and neighbor needs further clarification, however. Love is not well understood in our culture because it is often identified only with feelings and sexual desire. Love is defined in the dictionary as a strong emotional attachment characterized by tender feelings and devotion.[2] This still falls short of the biblical understanding, which depicts love as an action or something we do as well as feel.

Many of us began our lives as believers with a burst of enthusiasm and strong desire like a couple who have just married. Many young people go to a summer Christian camp and come home filled with renewed enthusiasm about following God only to find their zeal fading after being home for a few days. When feelings ebb and enthusiasm wanes, we find something else is needed to help us follow Christ. Some are puzzled by this while others often make this a matter of prayer, asking God for help, strength, and direction. One of the things God leads us to realize is that we cannot live for Him based on feelings alone.

What do we do when feelings fade and God seems far away? Ask any serious athlete about the importance of commitment. They spend many long hours training for an event that may last only a few seconds or minutes. It is commitment that takes us through the dry, desert experiences of life. Commitment leads us to act in love for God even in the ebb and flow of feelings.

Love is not only about warm fuzzies or good feelings. As Jesus said, it is a heart, soul, and mind commitment to act in loving ways toward God and others. Living in a commitment to express love is how we become holy and bring God glory. It is the choices we make each day in the ups and downs of life to be obedient to God and to act in love toward others.

This commitment is the glue in all our relationships. Only the commitment to act in love can give us stability in our relationships. It is a basic, key principle of living in God's kingdom. It is the central core of Christian ethics and it is how we can glorify God. This is how we become holy like Jesus. If we act in love, we can walk the different path in our world.

The best way to define or illustrate love is to look at God Himself. John, writing in his first epistle, gives us a good summary. We have seen earlier that 1 John 4:16 tells us, "God is love." 1 John 4:10 also states, "This is love: not that we loved God, but that he loved us and sent his Son as atoning sacrifice for our sins." First John 3:1 declares, "How great is the love the Father has lavished on us, that we should be called the children of God! And that is what we are!" And Jeremiah 31:3 assures us, "I have loved you with an everlasting love; I have drawn you with loving-kindness."

These and many other verses help us understand the nature of God's love. He is our heavenly Father who has an everlasting commitment to act in the best interests of those who choose to follow Him. God's dealings with the Israelites that are chronicled in the Old Testament tell the story of His unfailing love to an unfaithful people.

## Making the Commitment

We have seen the confusion and misunderstanding about love by an ungodly world. As believers we do not have to follow these misguided ideas. We do not have to live by a complex and contradictory list of rules. We do not have to live a shallow, unsatisfying life of self-indulgence. Instead, Jesus has given us a wonderful, positive principle of living in His kingdom. It is the gate to

God's "high way." It is the commitment to Jesus' principle of love that will pro-vide the stability needed to live in a confused world.

We can choose to make this commitment to act in love in all our relation-ships. It is not complicated. Just ask two simple questions. How can I express love to God? How can I express love to others? Our answer to these two ques-tions will determine the values and boundaries that will guide our lives. It is the key to how we become counter-cultural and build the kingdom of God.

This is what the church needs to tell the Patricks and Leenas in our congre-gations. The following chapters will help us learn in greater detail what love is like and how we can develop this foundational kingdom principle in our daily lives. Paul described it as "the most excellent way."

[1]*Merriam-Webster's Collegiate Dictionary*, Eleventh Edition (2003).
[2]Ibid.

## Further study, reflection, and discussion:

1.  Use the Scriptures in this chapter for more detailed personal or group study.
2.  How would you rate your commitment to live for God on a scale of 1-10?
3.  How does Matthew 12:1-14 illustrate the dangers of living by a set of rules?
4.  What does Philippians 3:18-19 tell us about people who make up their own rules?
5.  What did Jesus promise us in Matthew 11:28-30?

10

# The Guide Book

*Show me your ways, O Lord, teach me your paths; guide me in your truth and teach me, for you are God my Savior, and my hope is in you all day long* (Psalm 25:4-5).

The GPS has changed our lives. Whether walking or riding we can know where we are at all times on planet earth. We never have to be lost anymore, unless the battery dies. The only problem is the annoying voice that keeps saying, "Make a u-turn at the next intersection." Many golf courses have carts with a GPS device so golfers can know exactly how far it is to the green. It sure is helpful to know which club to use.

It would be wonderful to have a spiritual GPS to help guide and plan our daily lives and to make sound moral decisions. The fact is, this guide has been around far longer than the GPS. It has been giving guidance to believers for thousands of years. The Bible is the guide we can use as we make our journey of living in love for God and others. It doesn't need a battery. It just needs to be read, studied, and followed. It will help us find the boundaries and directions needed to discover how to live in moral excellence.

## Use the Guide Book

A GPS device will do us no good if it is left in a cabinet drawer or if we let the battery run down. Our Guide Book, the Bible, also will do us no good if it is left on the shelf to gather dust. A story is told of a mother who bought her five-year-old daughter a Bible story book only to find out that the little girl was circling the word God on each page. Deciding not to reprimand her for defacing her new book, the mother quietly asked, "Why are you doing that?" The little girl replied matter-of-factly, "So I will know where to find God when I need Him."[1]

If the Bible is where we find God speaking, what do our Bibles look like? Are they shiny, new, and clean, or do they bear the marks of frequent use? Do we underline verses that have spoken to our hearts or make notes in the margins we do not want to forget? A dog-eared Bible is usually a sign of its use in finding God.

Long ago Paul the Apostle gave the young man Timothy some advice in 2 Timothy 3:15-17,

> *From infancy you have known the holy Scriptures, which are able to make you wise for salvation through faith in Christ Jesus. All Scripture is God-breathed and is useful for teaching, rebuking, correcting and training in righteousness, so that the man of God may be thoroughly equipped for every good work.*

Paul was telling Timothy he had a Guide Book, a spiritual GPS that would guide him to learn what he needed to live a godly life. Like soldiers going into battle, we need to be thoroughly equipped to live a God inspired life.

A group of believers in Acts 17:11, the Bereans, were described as receiving "the message with great eagerness and examined the Scriptures every day to see if what Paul said was true." The picture is like that of investigators on the television program, CSI, who passionately look for clues to solve a mysterious crime. Let's imitate the Bereans. We too can put our hearts, souls, and minds into reading and studying our Guide Book. Doing this on a regular, daily schedule produces invaluable benefits for us.

We can pray for understanding and depend on the Holy Spirit for help as we study. Jesus promised in John 16:13, "But when he, the Spirit of truth, comes, he will guide you into all truth." The Holy Spirit will do this when we go to a church where the Scriptures are faithfully taught and preached. He will do this when we join with other believers in church-sponsored Bible studies and small groups. We do not need to be afraid to ask questions. As we all know, the only dumb question is the one we fail to ask. Mature believers will be glad to help us find answers. The Holy Spirit will be there to be our helper as well.

## Using the Old Testament

An important issue often ignored among believers needs to be addressed. Some people avoid reading the Old Testament because it seems so complicated and hard to understand. Others see it as outdated legalism that has been replaced by the New Testament. It is unfortunate to ignore the tremendous value the Old Testament has for us.

Biblical scholar Roger Nicole has noted this about the New Testament, "A very conservative count discloses unquestionably 295 references to the Old Testament. These occupy some 352 verses in the New Testament, or more than 4.4%."[2] This reminds us that the Old Testament was the Bible for Jesus and the early church. It is important for us to take another look at the Old Testament based on what Jesus said about love.

Earlier, we saw how Jesus' answer to the Pharisees in Matthew 22:34-40 was used to establish the foundation for a believer's behavior. We are to love God and our neighbor. He made an important comment in vs. 40, "All the Law and the Prophets hang on these two commandments." This short statement reveals what Jesus thought about the Old Testament. Then Paul repeated this in Romans 13:10 where he said, "Love is the fulfillment of the law." It is clear that Jesus and Paul both viewed the Old Testament Law through the prism of love. As such, the Old Testament is not to be hastily cast aside or ignored.

How are we to interpret the Old Testament? The book of Hebrews in the New Testament makes it clear that Jesus' death and resurrection fulfilled the priesthood and sacrifices put in place by Moses. We have already seen how Paul explained in Romans 13 the way love applies to the Ten Commandments. There are, however, many other Old Testament statements and stories we need to understand from the view of loving God and neighbor. A good passage in the Old Testament illustrating this can be found in Leviticus 18 and 19. Take some time to read through these chapters.

Moses spoke to the Israelites in Leviticus 19:2, giving the reason for God's commands. He said, "Be holy because I, the Lord your God, am holy." Peter used this in his first New Testament letter (1 Peter 1:15-16) to say the same thing to believers. God's goal for His people has always been holiness, to be like Him. Leviticus 18 and 19 makes it clear that the Israelites were to be different from their surrounding neighbors in their behavior and appearance.

Chapter 18 deals with unlawful sexual relations, which we would characterize today as simple common sense to prevent family and social chaos. Chapter 19 deals with a variety of laws, some which repeat the Ten Commandments. Some are very practical and not outdated at all. Verse 16 is a good example, "Do not go about spreading slander among your people. Do not do anything that endangers your neighbor's life." Slander and reckless endangerment are written into our legal code today.

While some of Moses' commands applied only to the culture of that day, the underlying principles are still valid for believers in all ages. These principles offer us truths to help us evaluate our love for God and others.

A good example is the often misunderstood Old Testament practice of tithing. It is mentioned numerous times throughout the Old Testament, culminating in the declaration in Malachi 3:8-12 where the Israelites were accused of robbing God by withholding their tithe. Some dismiss tithing as an outdated legal requirement, declaring we are no longer under law but under grace. But if we are to be guided by our love of God, what standard are we to use to measure our giving? Are we just to decide what we think we can give? We all know what happens when we set our own standards.

The Old Testament practice of tithing gives us a good pattern or standard to use. The next time we give an offering in church, we can ask ourselves, "How much am I expressing my love for God?" The principle of tithing will help us find the answer.

The basic principle of the Old Testament, living a holy life by expressing love to God and others, is timeless in its relevance. Read and study the Old Testament through the eyes and understanding of Jesus. If He thought them to be important then so should we. We will see the Old Testament in a new way. And we will better understand the teachings of the New Testament as well. There is much for us to learn from the Old Testament laws and from the history of the Israelites. It is there for our benefit and instruction.

## Applying Both Testaments

Deuteronomy 19:14 gave an interesting command to the Israelites, "Do not move your neighbor's boundary stone set up by your predecessors in the inheritance you received in the land the Lord your God is giving you to possess." These boundary stones were important in keeping public order and preserving a person's inheritance.

Boundaries are important in all of life. All sports have them. Hitting a golf ball out of bounds costs a player a penalty stroke. Valuable points can be lost in many sports because players step out of bounds. God wants to set boundaries to give our lives order and to preserve our spiritual inheritance in Christ. The Bible will tell us where to set these boundaries. It will guide us in living a rewarding, productive, and fulfilling life of moral excellence.

It is important to use the entire Bible, both Old and New Testaments. We need to learn what a passage or story actually says. It is also important to determine what it meant to the people of that day. We also will want to understand what the passage reveals about God and human nature. Having done that, we can ask what basic underlying principle is found in the passage or story that will help us express love to God or our neighbor.

Second Peter 1:19 states, "We have the word of the prophets made more certain, and you do well to pay attention to it, as a light shining in a dark place, until the day dawns and the morning star rises in your hearts." The Bible will be our source of wisdom to help us live for God until Jesus returns. It will give us the encouragement and strength to face the influences and challenges of a godless world.

The Scriptures can become an integral part of our daily lives, giving us the guidance we need and desire. Our children can learn the Bible from the primary influence in their lives—Dad and Mom. They can learn life's boundaries by listening to us and watching us live out the truths of the Bible in our daily lives. This is how the next generation learns to have faith in God and to follow His ways as they grow to adulthood.

Most of us have bought furniture that needs to be assembled. Some of us think we are smart enough to do it without reading the directions. Inevitably, after wasting much time, we end up having to read the directions to get it right.

Books like this one may be helpful, but only the Bible, both Old and New Testaments, will provide the necessary instructions sorely needed to get it right. The Holy Spirit will use our Guide Book to help us. Like a GPS device, it will give us the directions needed to get where God wants us to be. It will also tell us when we are headed in the wrong direction.

Those who do not have a Bible can purchase one such as the *New International Version* or the *New Living Translation*. Several other versions are available also. There is no need to lose our way if we use our Guide Book to lead us to moral excellence.

[1]Michael P. Green, Ed., *Illustrations for Biblical Preaching* (Grand Rapids: Baker Book House, 1989), 34-35.
[2]Roger Nicole, *Revelation and the Bible*, ed. Carl F. H. Henry (Grand Rapids: Baker, 1958), p. 137.

## Further study, reflection, and discussion:

1. Use the Scriptures in this chapter for more detailed personal or group study
2. Why should you have a systematic plan to read through the Bible?
3. What does the term inspiration mean? Use a Bible dictionary for help.
4. What can we learn from Ephesians 6:10-20 about being spiritually equipped?
5. Have you ever read through the Old Testament? Why? Why not?
6. What group do you attend to study the Bible with other believers? Why? Why not?
7. What are some of the ways you can teach your children the Bible?

11

# Thinking the Thoughts of God

*How precious to me are your thoughts, O God! How vast is the sum of them! Were I to count them, they would outnumber the grains of sand* (Psalm 139:17-18).

The term, "politically correct," entered our world in the '70s. The speech police have been increasingly active ever since. The emphasis in our society on multiculturalism has led to the renaming of many things found to be negative and offensive. Almost every day brings new examples. Some are quite creative and even funny, while others seem silly or ridiculous. People who were called clumsy are now referred to as uniquely coordinated. Instead of being called incompetent, a person is specially skilled. We are no longer allowed to use the word *worse*. Instead we say least best.[1]

Progressives seek to change the way we think and speak about a wide variety topics. This raises important questions for us. Why do we think and speak the way we do? Where do we get our values to decide what is right or wrong? How can we develop the right ideas about love of God and others that lead to moral excellence?

## The Battle for Our Minds

Previously we looked at the major belief systems that have shaped our culture. We think the way we do because we were raised and educated under the influence of these ideas. We developed a mindset or a fixed mental attitude formed by our genes and by our experiences from family, education, and constant daily contact with our culture. This determines our values and shapes every aspect of our lives.

Because it is so deeply imbedded in our minds, little thought is given to our mindset. It is accepted without question as fact. This is why we think others are odd when they do not think and act as we do. Our individual mindsets cause us to see things differently. This becomes even more obvious when we associate with those from other cultures. If you have been to another country, you no doubt have experienced some degree of culture shock.

Understanding our mindset as sinners is very important for believers. Harry

Blamires wrote several years ago, "There is no longer a Christian mind."[2] His remarks remind us of the uncomfortable reality of our mindsets. The truth is that many of us are content to know we are saved but give little thought to changing the way we think.

It is unfortunate that some of us neglect our minds. We try to live the Christian life using the enemy's ideas. It is like trying to swim upstream with our hands tied only to be swept along by a force that it far stronger than us. Trying to live this way is self-defeating, discouraging, and unsatisfying. The impact of our lives for God and His kingdom is seriously compromised as well.

We are in a battle for our hearts and minds in our culture today. Paul warned in Colossians 2:8, "See to it that no one takes you captive through hollow and deceptive philosophy, which depends on human tradition and the basic principles of this world rather than on Christ." It's still good advice.

Accepting Christ as our Savior is just the beginning. As believers something must begin to change. When people join the military, they are sent to boot camp. The military knows they have to change the way recruits think if they are to function as soldiers. Boot camp begins that process with sudden reality.

Surrounded by a godless culture, we need to establish new values, make different decisions, and relate to others and to God in ways which we previously did not know. We can develop a new mindset, a Christian mind that learns to think and act in love to God and others. It is vital to grasp the importance of this and enter the battle to change the way we think. It is the only way we can achieve moral excellence.

Developing a Christian mind requires understanding the impact of sin on our minds. Isaiah 55:8-9 warns us,

*"My thoughts are not your thoughts, neither are your ways my ways," declares the Lord. "As the heavens are higher than the earth, so are my ways higher than your ways, and my thoughts than your thoughts."*

Paul stated in Romans 8:7-8,

*The sinful mind is hostile to God. It does not submit to God's law nor can it do so. Those controlled by the sinful nature cannot please God.*

We have a problem. Our minds are infected with a deadly spiritual disease called sin. Only God has the cure wrapped up in the person and work of Christ Jesus. Only He can fill the God-hole in our lives. Only He can replace our dysfunction with His wholeness. The process to do this must include our minds.

# Metamorphosis

Watching science programs on television reveals remarkable things about nature. I recently watched a fascinating video showing the stunning development in fast speed time of a caterpillar turning into a gorgeous butterfly. This is a great illustration of what will take place as we make a commitment to change the way we think.

Paul gives us the key in Romans 12:1-2,

*Therefore, I urge you, brothers, in view of God's mercy, to offer your bodies as living sacrifices, holy and pleasing to God—this is your spiritual act of worship. Do not conform any longer to the pattern of this world, but be transformed by the renewing of your mind. Then you will be able to test and approve what God's will is—his good, pleasing and perfect will.*

The word translated *offer* reflects the Old Testament practice of animal sacrifices. An animal obviously could only be offered once, but Paul's use of the words *living sacrifice* tells us that we are to live our lives at all times in submission to God's will and way. It is a daily walk. The "hungering and thirsting for righteousness" in Matthew 5:6 emphasizes the desire that motivates us to make this commitment.

The word translated *transformed* is where we get the word *metamorphosis,* which we use to describe how an ugly caterpillar turns into a beautiful butterfly. Paul is clear that this transformation is in our minds.

As we daily commit or offer ourselves to this process, we can be transformed from secular thinkers into those who think the thoughts of God. This is an important part of achieving our goal of becoming like Jesus. It will not happen overnight, but this commitment is vital and will change our lives. It will be challenging but enormously rewarding as we learn to live in moral excellence.

As was mentioned in chapter one, learning to live a godly life is not just an intellectual process. God's truth must not only be understood, it must be internalized. This means it must have a heart, soul, and mind impact on us. It needs to get inside us and affect the way we think and live every day. Using the butterfly analogy, we need to be changed from the inside out.

## Our Helper

It is important to realize that this is not a self-help, pull-yourself-up-by-the-boot-straps approach. In fact, we cannot do this by ourselves. As previously noted, we quickly discover we lack bootstraps. We will need God's help to follow His commands. Thankfully, He does not leave us alone to muddle along as best we can.

John 14:15-17 illustrates this command/promise for us. First, Jesus said, "If you love me, you will obey what I command." He followed this with, "And I will ask the Father, and he will give you another Counselor to be with you forever—the Spirit of truth." The word *counselor* can be translated as one called alongside to help. Jesus' command to obey is connected to the provision of help that will enable us to be obedient.

Some people today are employing personal trainers to help them keep in shape physically. Imagine having a personal spiritual coach and teacher. This is exactly what God has given each of us. The Holy Spirit is our teacher who provides guidance and strength. He inspired the Bible for our instruction. He uses other believers to support us in prayer and to help us understand what the Bible teaches. He uses what we learn to speak to our consciences, bringing conviction to our hearts when we have sinned.

## The Right Focus

Many people who have never worn glasses find that they need them around the age of forty to keep things in proper focus. Our lives are like eye glasses with the wrong focus because of sin. Developing a Christian mind requires us to change our focus from the things that characterized our lives as non-believers.

Paul addressed this in Romans 8:5 where he said, "Those who live according to the sinful nature have their minds set on what that nature desires; but those who live in accordance with the Spirit have their minds set on what the Spirit desires." Character matters to the Holy Spirit. He wants us to bring moral excellence into focus in our daily lives.

We can also think of our minds as gardens where weeds are always a problem. Left unattended, a garden will be overtaken by them. As a gardener, I have learned to use mulch or a fabric weed blocker that lets the rain through but keeps the weeds from sprouting. As believers, with the help of the Holy Spirit, we can block the old sinful thoughts and plant the new thoughts of God. Philippians 4:8 gives us important advice for our minds. "Finally, brothers, whatever is true, whatever is noble, whatever is right, whatever is pure, whatever is lovely, whatever is admirable—if anything is excellent or praiseworthy—think about such things."

Studying and memorizing Bible verses as well as singing Christian songs are good ways to plant good thoughts in our minds. Paul urged believers in Colossians 3:1-2,

*Since, then, you have been raised with Christ, set your hearts on things above where Christ is seated at the right hand of God. Set your minds on things above, not on earthly things.*

We are in a battle for control of the way we think. Our minds have been affected by our sinful nature and influenced by a secular culture. The good news is we can have our minds transformed from the old patterns by focusing on those things that are pleasing to God. We have been given a divine helper, the Holy Spirit, who will be with us in this process of changing the way we think.

Using our Guide Book, the Bible, we can take time each day to learn and think about Christian virtues and how they can be applied in our lives. Fellow believers will give us encouragement and share what they have learned. We can begin the adventure today of thinking the thoughts of God. It is the way we learn to excel in our world.

[1]bored.com/pcphrases. Accessed July 16, 2011.
[2]Harry Blamires, *The Christian Mind* (Ann Arbor. MI.: Servant, 1963), 3.

## Further study, reflection, and discussion:

1. Use the Scriptures in this chapter for more detailed personal or group study.
2. What experiences or people have greatly influenced the way you view God, life, right and wrong, relationships, money, etc.?
3. How often during the day do your thoughts turn to God and how He would have you live?
4. What influences your mind at present—books, magazines, TV programs, hobbies, recreation, internet, etc.?
5. How much time do you give to personal Bible study, prayer, and fellowship with other believers?

12

# Love in All the Wrong Places

*Do your best to come to me quickly, for Demas, because he loved this world, has deserted me and has gone to Thessalonica* (2 Timothy 4:9-10).

A bank in Texas put up the following billboard advertisement, "We Lend Happiness at Eighteen Locations." Sounds enticing, doesn't it? If winners of millions in state lotteries are any indication, nothing could be further from the truth. Studies indicate the winners are not prepared to deal with the pressures and demands that come with winning. Many of their lives have been marked by tragedy. Most of us will never win a lottery, but our lives can still be affected by the pursuit of money.

## The Love of Money

Paul put it this way when he counseled Timothy in 1 Timothy 6:9-10,

*People who want to get rich fall into temptation and a trap and into many foolish and harmful desires that plunge men into ruin and destruction. For the love of money is a root of all kinds of evil. Some people, eager for money, have wandered from the faith and pierced themselves with many griefs.*

It almost seems as though Paul knew a few lottery winners. Notice that Paul says the problem is not money itself but rather the love of money.

The love of money can affect everyone, even the poorest among us. Poverty drives some people to crime and others to waste their income by spending it on things they really cannot afford. Their desire for what they do not have leads them "into ruin and destruction." Atlantic City, New Jersey, glows at night with the glitter of casinos and the promise of hitting the jackpot. What is not seen are the people sleeping under the boardwalk after losing all their money.

Some people who are wealthy still pursue money, and in seeking more and more, fall into the same trap. How can we navigate the treacherous pitfalls of money? Understanding the purpose of money and wealth from a biblical perspective is important if we are to excel in our world.

Paul gave us a key insight writing in 1 Timothy 6:17-19, He stated,

*Command those who are rich in this present world not to be arrogant nor to put their hope in wealth, which is so uncertain, but to put their hope in God, who richly provides us with everything for our enjoyment. Command them to do good, to be rich in good deeds, and to be generous and willing to share. In this way they will lay up treasure for themselves as a firm foundation for the coming age, so that they may take hold of the life that is truly life.*

Paul is saying the way to deal with money is to have the correct attitude and perspective. He uses the word arrogant to describe someone who has the attitude they have acquired their wealth themselves. They put their hope in their wealth. Paul says this is fraught with uncertainty.

Alonzo had a good job in marketing, making a great salary. However, he spent his evenings partying and enjoying the night life. Along the way he began sampling the drugs that were readily available. Alonzo was soon hooked and eventually lost his job. His job and money were gone. He ended up sleeping under an expressway overpass and eating one meal a day at a soup kitchen. Fortunately, this story had a happy ending when Alonzo found a Christian drug rehabilitation center.

If God chooses to bless a person with wealth, Paul says there is a two-fold purpose for it. First, we are to use our wealth to be a blessing and help to others by being generous and willing to share. Using our money to bless the advancement of God's kingdom by supporting the local church, evangelistic outreaches, helping the needy, Christian colleges, overseas missions programs, and many other Christian ministries accomplishes this goal.

Secondly, we are to use our wealth to lay up treasures for the life to come. It is not about getting as much money as we can in this life. It is about impacting the world to come by preparing for eternity. All the money we can accumulate in this life will be left behind when we die. The only thing that will matter is whether or not we used that money to lay up treasure in heaven. The real results of our money will be revealed in the life to come. The results will most likely surprise us.

Paul concludes by showing the results of using money this way, "so that they may take hold of the life that is truly life." Quality over quantity matters. Many believers who are poor by worldly standards have learned the grace and blessing of giving.

A believer who has the right attitude and perspective toward money will have a life "that is truly life." Managing and using our money wisely leads us toward this life of quality. Used in the right way, money can enhance the life of the giver as well as blessing others. Money is not an end in itself; it is one of the means we can use to live in love toward God and others.

What about those who have very little money? This was true for most of the people of Jesus' day. It is still true in our day, especially in third world countries. Worry about the lack of money can eat away at the quality of life.

Tough financial times can be challenging for believers. Sickness or the loss of a job can be financially crippling. Sometimes we bring these problems on ourselves by overspending and mismanaging our money. The stresses can seem overwhelming at times. (There is help available in the Christian community. For example, counseling from a Christian perspective for financial problems is available from Crown Financial Ministries at www.crown.org or Dave Ramsey at www.daveramsey.com.)

Lack of money is where the rubber meets the road in trusting God. It is one of the tests of where we put our treasure and focus our love. Jesus addressed this problem in Matthew 6:31-33,

*So do not worry, saying, "What shall we eat?" or "What shall we drink?" or "What shall we wear?" For the pagans run after all these things, and your heavenly Father knows that you need them. But seek first his kingdom and his righteousness, and all these things will be given to you as well.*

If we have the proper attitude and perspective about money and giving, Paul gave this promise in Philippians 4:19, "And my God will meet all your needs according to his glorious riches in Christ Jesus." If we love God, we will learn to trust Him when our finances are tight. Putting God above money or the lack thereof is the way to excel in our world.

## Loving the World

Love of money has roots that go deeper than we may be aware. It is not always about the dollar bill. A small boy with his grandmother was observed in a department store crying as if his heart were broken. He was not a happy camper. The problem—his Grammy had refused to let him buy a toy he had seen. Someone has said the only difference between a boy and a man is the size of his toys. Girls and women have similar issues too.

We live in a world saturated with stuff. There's all kinds of food, entertainment, sports, or hobbies, for example. It is easy for the believer to become caught up in all of this. Without thinking we can find ourselves becoming possessed by our possessions and captives of our culture.

A strong warning about the "foolish and harmful desires that plunge men into ruin and destruction" is given in 1 John 2:15-17.

*Do not love the world or anything in the world. If anyone loves the world, the love of the Father is not in him. For everything in the world—the cravings of sinful man, the lust of his eyes and the boasting of what he has and does—comes not from the Father but from the world. The world and its desires pass away, but the man who does the will of God lives forever.*

It is important to explain John's use of the word *world* in order for us to get the full impact of what he is saying. He is not referring to the physical world, but to the world outside God's kingdom, the other kingdom where Satan rules. All those outside God's kingdom were viewed as being under the rule of sin and evil. John saw it as a godless kingdom with corrupted values and gods.

John continues by talking about three things that characterize the world of evil. First, he mentions in verse 16 "the cravings of sinful man." All of us have natural human desires. John is referring to the condition in which the normal desires are used outside the boundaries God has set. It may be as simple as gorging ourselves at the local smorgasbord. It can be as serious as Alonzo, who let his cravings get out of control and ended up sleeping under an overpass. For the believer it is a matter of staying within God's boundaries. When these desires become unbridled and out-of-control, they produce grave consequences.

Our culture is afflicted with many kinds of addictions. 1 Peter 1:13 tells us, "Therefore, prepare your minds for action; be self-controlled." Paul also gave us some good advice in Galatians 5:16, "So I say, live by the Spirit, and you will not gratify the desires of the sinful nature." Since the Holy Spirit is characterized as the believer's divine helper, we can look to Him for help in keeping our physical cravings under control.

Next, John mentions in verse 16, "the lust of the eyes." The advertising industry is well aware of this human trait. A recent commercial attracted viewers with, "I want it all! I want it now!" What we see is what we want. We are just like the young child in the department store with his grandmother.

The Federal Reserve Board's figures recently announced a total credit card debt in the United States of $972,494,000—almost one trillion dollars. It goes up almost every year. At the root of this is materialism, the desire for more and more things and the latest and greatest, most up-to-date gadget. McMansions is a term recently coined to describe the size of homes once thought only for the wealthy. The recent 2008 housing market crash is a good example of the results of the desire for more and more. Jesus gave this warning in Luke 12:15, "Watch out! Be on your guard against all kinds of greed; a man's life does not consist in the abundance of his possessions."

Finally, John mentions in verse 16 "the boasting of what one has and does." A clever salesman tapped into this attitude closing hundreds of sales with this line: "Let me show you something several of your neighbors said you couldn't afford." Pride is the crown of physical cravings and lust of the eyes. Notice how the commercials for expensive cars appeal to our pride. We are encouraged to park the car in our driveway with pride. We can arrive at our friends' homes to the sound of their "oohs" and "aahs" of envy.

Jesus has a surprise in store for people who take pride in their possessions. He declared in Matthew 5:5 that only the meek would inherit the earth. One day when Christ's kingdom comes in full array, those filled with pride will be on the outside. Those who build their lives around kingdom values will come into an inheritance far, far more glorious than the temporary things of this world which are destined to pass away. Possessions do not satisfy the deep longing in our hearts for significance and worth. Living a God-inspired life is the only way to fill this need.

John concludes with this statement in verse 17, "but the man who does the will of God lives forever." Godly living not only pays dividends in this life, it also leads us ultimately to eternal life.

The bank in Texas had it wrong. Money does not bring true happiness. As believers we can successfully confront the siren call of money, the craving for more possessions, and the desire for all we can see along with pride in possessing it all. Failure to confront these desires puts love in all the wrong places. As believers we can choose to live by values that are eternal. Living in love for God will help us resist the attraction and pull of a materialist culture. It is how we can live in our world without becoming captured by its temporary pleasures. It is another way we can excel in our world.

## Further study, reflection, and discussion:

1. Use the Scriptures in this chapter for more detailed personal or group study.
2. How should our love of God affect how we spend money?
3. Should we have a financial budget? Why? Why not?
4. How much and what kind of debt is permitted for a believer?
5. If Satan is the ruler of this present world, what are the implications for us as believers?
6. What limits should we place on having fun and seeking pleasure?
7. How can we know when we have been captured by our possessions even those we do not have yet?

13

# Put Off—Put On

*Hate what is evil; cling to what is good* (Romans 12:9).

Molly and Fred were watching their favorite television program along with their two children, Butch and Sandy. It was hilarious and everyone was splitting their sides laughing. As usual, the time for commercials arrived. Suddenly they were confronted by a new commercial that should have been x-rated. They searched frantically for the remote, but the damage was done. Molly and Fred knew questions would soon follow. What could they say to their children?

Because it sells, the media and entertainment world pushes sex, foul language, and violence. Adult items are routinely advertised on television at all hours. It is not only children who are adversely affected. Our senses are bombarded with this constantly. It has a cumulative effect on all of us. Movies cleverly depict all this as desirable but omit the consequences. Many computer games do the same. The list goes on and on. The coarsening of our world continues unabated. The nature of our morally bankrupt culture cries out for an answer to the tide of evil that seeks to overwhelm us. What are we to do? What is love's attitude toward sin?

## Put off the Old

Paul addressed the believer's attitude toward evil in Ephesians 4:22 where he said, "You were taught, with your former way of life, to put off your old self, which is being corrupted by its deceitful desires."

Colossians 3:5 uses strong language to make the same point, "Put to death, therefore, whatever belongs to your earthly nature."

First Peter 2:1 puts it like this, "Therefore, rid yourselves of all malice and deceit, hypocrisy, envy, and slander of every kind." The word *rid* is used of putting off one's clothing. The picture is that of a beggar taking off ragged and dirty clothes. Strong phrases like *put to death* describe the focus and commitment we are to have in our hearts and minds toward sin and evil. The best answer to the media is the off button.

The Bible identifies specific attitudes and behaviors along with strong warnings in numerous passages. Paul stated in Galatians 5:19-21,

*The acts of the sinful nature are obvious: sexual immorality, impurity and debauchery; idolatry and witchcraft; hatred, discord, jealousy, fits of rage, selfish ambition, dissensions, factions and envy; drunkenness, orgies, and the like. I warn you, as I did before, that those who live like this will not inherit the kingdom.*

Our attitudes and actions toward evil are clearly laid out in these and other passages.

The warnings are clear. God's judgment will come on those who choose to live by the sinful patterns of our culture. This may sound like fire and brimstone to some, but as believers, we cannot ignore what God says in His Word. We cannot pick and choose only the parts we like. We do so at our peril. The stakes are enormous and have eternal consequences.

Paul went on to say in Ephesians 5:8-12,

*For you were once in darkness, but now you are light in the Lord. Live as children of light (for the fruit of the light consists in all goodness, righteousness and truth) and find out what pleases the Lord. Have nothing to do with the fruitless deeds of darkness, but rather expose them.*

This does not mean we publish our neighbor's sins on Facebook or on our blog. Yes, the old cliché is still true, we are to love the sinner but hate the sin. What it means is the quality of our daily lives should stand in marked contrast to the culture around us. This is an area of our lives where we need to give serious thought concerning how much we reflect the world dominated by ungodly ideas. We are not meant to mirror our culture but to reflect the Lord Jesus. It is how God wants us to live in excellence.

One area that needs special attention is the addictions that have plagued the lives of people before coming to Christ. Try as they might, some people cannot break free on their own. Many people need special help to break the hold these addictions have on their lives. There are clinics and centers in almost every community offering counseling and assistance from a biblical perspective. Most pastors of local churches can help people find an appropriate place.

Centers like Teen Challenge, Youth Challenge, and other Christian based programs have helped many people recover from drug and alcohol addiction. The *12 Step Program* developed by Alcoholics Anonymous has been adapted by numerous programs to a wide variety of addictions. Many churches provide recovery groups where people share their stories and provide mutual support. If our churches do not have these groups, we can work with our pastors to start one. The power of these addictions can be broken with God's help and the loving care provided by fellow believers. A person does not have to struggle alone in putting off the old life.

## Put on the New

Paul gave believers the second part of the equation when it comes to living in a godless culture. He tells us in Ephesians 4:24, "Put on the new self, created to be like God in true righteousness and holiness." He lets us know the process of putting off sin is to be balanced by the continuing effort to build into our lives those things that are pleasing to God. The outlook and attitude of love will have positive effects on our lives.

Paul emphasized the development of godly virtues in our lives in Colossians 3:12-17,

> *Therefore, as God's chosen people, holy and dearly loved, clothe your-*
> *selves with compassion, kindness, humility, gentleness and patience.*
> *Bear with each other and forgive whatever grievances you may have*
> *against one another. Forgive as the Lord forgave you. And over all*
> *these virtues put on love, which binds them all together in perfect unity.*

The word translated *clothe* here in Colossians captures the picture of putting on new clothes. Women as well as some men like to indulge in retail therapy. We all like to buy new clothes. As believers we can have spiritual therapy as we clothe ourselves in spiritual garments.

Paul mentioned in Galatians 5:22-23, "But the fruit if the Spirit is love, joy, peace, patience, kindness, goodness, faithfulness, gentleness and self-control." These are the things the Holy Spirit wants to produce in our lives.

Paul also stated in Romans 8:5,

> *Those who live according to the sinful nature have their minds set on*
> *what that nature desires; but those who live in accordance with the*
> *Spirit have their minds set on what the Spirit desires.*

We have been described as having a wolf and a lamb inside of us. We can choose which one to feed. That is why it is so important to read, study, and meditate on God's Word, the Bible.

Proverbs 4:6 tells us, "Do not forsake wisdom, and she will protect you; love her, and she will watch over you." Paul gave us some good advice in Ephesians 5:15-16,

> *Be very careful, the, how you live—not as unwise but as wise, making*
> *the most of every opportunity, because the days are evil.*

Love and wisdom are partners in living a God inspired life. J.I. Packer put it this way, "Wisdom is the power to see and the inclination to choose the best and highest goal, together with the surest means of attaining it."[1]

Your Guide Book is the source of God's wisdom. James 1:5 assures us, "If any of you lack wisdom, he should ask God, who gives generously to all without finding fault, and it will be given to him." Prayer is the place to ask.

Jesus taught us in Matthew 7:7, "Ask and it will be given to you; seek and you will find; knock and the door will be opened to you." The words used indicate persistence; ask and keep on asking, seek and keep on seeking, knock and keep on knocking.

These virtues cannot be developed in a vacuum. It is not enough to study and talk about Christian character. These virtues will only be developed by actually applying them where we live. We are with people all the time—family, friends, neighbors, coworkers, even the check-out clerk. This is where godly character really counts.

It is easy to show kindness to those we like and who like us. Most of us struggle impatiently in a slow check-out line or a traffic jam. The real test comes when we are placed in situations with people who irritate us, disagree with us, and in general make our lives unpleasant. Since love is a choice to act in a certain way, we can choose how to respond.

Someone discovered many years ago that we can teach canaries how to sing by putting them in a cage with a nightingale. A more up-to-date approach plays a recording of our voice to teach a canary or parakeet to talk. The question we need to ask is, "How much does our love influence the lives of those around us?" Like the nightingale, what song do we sing as believers?

Perhaps Paul's most well known list of the characteristics of love is found in 1 Corinthians 13:4-7,

> *Love is patient, love is kind. It does not envy, it does not boast, it is not proud. It is not rude, it is not self-seeking, it is not easily angered, it keeps no record of wrongs. Love does not delight in evil but rejoices with the truth. It always protects, always trusts, always hopes, always perseveres.*

These are the songs we can sing in our daily lives as we live in our world. Just think of the influence we can have if we began to put these things into practice.

Molly and Fred have the resources to teach their children the godly way of living. We do too. As believers we can begin the process of putting off the old tattered rags of sinful living and putting on the new clothes of godly attitudes and behavior.

Our Guide Book has many passages and stories of Bible characters which teach the positive virtues to build into our lives. Both good and bad examples of living are found there. We can pray for the help of the Holy Spirit in developing godly character where we live each day. It is the way we can excel in our world.

[1]J. I. Packer, *Knowing God* (Downers Grove: Intervarsity Press, 1973), p. 80.

## Further study, reflection, and discussion:

1. Use the Scriptures in this chapter for further personal or group study. A Bible dictionary will be helpful to look up individual words.
2. What do you learn from Ephesians 4:17 – 5:21 about sinful attitudes and behavior?
3. What do you learn from Proverbs 6:16-19 about tolerating evil?
4. What kind of activities with your children can you substitute for watching television, movies and computer games?
5. How should you react to the sinful behavior of those with whom you associate on a daily basis?
6. What Christian programs are available in your area to help those with addictions?

14

# Who Is Our Hero?

*"Come, follow me," Jesus said* (Matthew 4:19).

Our culture makes heroes of entertainment and sports figures. Entertainers like Elvis Presley and Michael Jackson have been enshrined with almost god-like status even though they lived tortured personal lives. We seldom hear about people like Billy Graham or Mother Teresa mentioned as role models. Though they are admired, there is no market for tee shirts, sneakers, or other items with their endorsements.

Two thousand eighth grade students were asked whom they would choose as their hero. As you would expect, the most often selected were all entertainers and sports figures. We may be quick to dismiss this based on the age of the students, but the truth is that we adults are not far removed from these students in some respects.

We also have our heroes and idols. Expensive sports jerseys and designer clothing with just the right label attract our dollars. Look at the way people dress at a game or party. We even walk and talk a certain way. Some people have spent thousands of dollars buying memorabilia of their favorite hero or team. As believers we need to ask ourselves, "Who is our hero or role model? Whom do we imitate? Who is really worthy of being our hero?"

## A Worthy Hero

The word *disciple* is used frequently in the New Testament. It describes a person who was a learner-follower of a teacher or rabbi. Disciples would not only learn from the teacher but would try to pattern their lives after him. As believers we are called as Jesus' disciples to imitate Him, to pattern our lives after Him. What does this mean for us?

John 3:16 tells us, "For God so love the world that he gave his one and only Son, that whoever believes in him shall not perish by have eternal life." Since Jesus was the expression God's love to the world, we are also called to imitate Christ. Jesus gave this command in John 15:12, "Love each other as I have loved you."

Paul gave us some specifics of how we can so this in Philippians 2:3-8.

*Do nothing out of selfish ambition or vain conceit, but in humility con-sider others better than yourselves. Each of you should look not only to your own interests, but also to the interests of others. Your attitude should be the same as that of Christ Jesus: Who being in very nature God, did not consider equality with God something to be grasped, but made himself nothing, taking the very nature of a servant, he humbled himself and became obedient to death—even death on a cross!*

Jesus, with great courage, loved us out of a humble, selfless spirit. He is our Hero. He alone is worthy. His unselfish, humble giving of Himself is our basic pattern for loving others. It will lead us to move from a selfish, me-centered way of life to one where we consider the interests and needs of others.

## Applied Humility

William Temple described humility this way, "Humility is not thinking less of yourself than of other people, nor does it mean having a low opinion of your own gifts. It means freedom from thinking about yourself at all."

Paul declared in Ephesians 4:1-3,

*As a prisoner of the Lord, I urge you to live a life worthy of the calling you have received. Be completely humble and gentle; be patient, bearing with one another in love. Make every effort to keep the unity of the Spirit through the bond of peace.*

He encouraged believers in Romans 12:10, "Be devoted to one another in brotherly love. Honor one another above yourselves."

As we read and study Paul's letters, we will find he had to deal with the is-sues of personal relationships in the churches where believers were at odds over a variety of problems. He made the point to the Romans and Ephesians that gentle humility is meant to change the dynamics of how we respond to others. Paul's use of the Greek word translated *make every effort* indicates the energy we are to put into developing this attitude in our lives. We may not be able to change the other person, but we can change ourselves with God's help.

Gentle humility is not easy. Our sinful nature tends to make us self-centered and selfish. What happens when someone offends us in some way? How do we respond? Even if we do not respond in kind, do we still harbor feelings of unforgiving resentment? This is how our relationships deteriorate into long term anger and tit-for-tat responses. Bad blood continues long after the original event. It's the Hatfields and the McCoys all over again. Our lists of grievances grow longer and longer. A change of heart is needed when we fall into this trap.

Paul spoke to these issues in Romans 12:14-21. He stated in verse 14, "Bless those who persecute you; bless and do not curse." Doing this takes us out of the cycle of getting even. We are to make an honest, humble effort to get along with everyone. He says in verse 18 that we are to do our part, "If it is possible, as far as it depends on you, live at peace with everyone." We are to "leave room for God's wrath" by putting others in His hands not ours.

Paul quotes from Proverbs 25:21-22 in verse 20, "If your enemy is hungry, feed him; if he is thirsty, give him something to drink. In doing this, you will heap burning coals on his head." He concludes by declaring, "Do not be overcome by evil, but overcome evil with good."

Harry had an irate customer coming to the car dealership where he worked. A mistake had been made when the customer brought their car in for servicing. The oil cap had not been replaced properly and had come off while they were driving. Oil was all over the engine compartment. How could Harry handle this angry customer?

When we know we will have to deal with an awkward relationship, we can prepare by asking for the strength and wisdom of the Holy Spirit. Then we can enter the situation with the commitment to be humble and gentle. We can prepare to apologize for our part in the disagreement. We can also change our tone of voice along with the words and expressions we use. We can choose not to get into another word battle and we can release the desire to win the argument or justify ourselves.

Harry got it right by apologizing and cleaning the engine. He even gave the customer a free oil change. The customer could have gone to another shop, but because of Harry's humble response, he returned faithfully.

Paul is saying we have a responsibility to change the dynamics of our relationships by changing ourselves. It is not about winning or losing, it is about imitating Jesus. The benefits are enormous if we commit ourselves to work gentle humility into our lives—with the emphasis on work.

## Reaching Out

Jesus did more than just express gentle humility by dying on the cross. He also expressed God's love while He was still alive by pouring His life into His followers, especially the twelve. He changed their lives by leaving an indelible imprint on their hearts, souls, and minds. We too will leave an imprint. We can imitate what Jesus did as we express His love to those around us.

Numerous times in the Gospels He showed compassion toward those who were not considered worthy. Matthew 8:1-4 tells how Jesus actually touched a leper as He healed him. Matthew 9:9-13 describes Jesus' call of Matthew, a despised tax collector. Luke 19:1-10 shows Him reaching out to Zacchaeus, another tax collector. Matthew 14:14 states that when the crowds followed His boat to a solitary place, "When Jesus landed and saw a large crowd, he had compassion on them and healed their sick." It was here that He fed 5,000 men plus women and children.

John 4 tells us of His contact with the Samaritan woman at the well in Sychar. Even His disciples expressed surprise that He was talking with her, a hated female Samaritan. These stories of Jesus give us a powerful example of how we can express God's love by reaching out to those rejected and despised by everyone else. People like this are all around us. We can look for them and reach out to them in love. It's what Jesus did.

Expressing the love of God was Jesus' commitment. His determination is summarized by His prayer in Gethsemane. Matthew 26:36-46 records that He prayed three times, "My Father, if it is possible, may this cup be taken from me. Yet not as I will, but as you will."

Jesus' humanity exerted itself just like us as we try to express God's love in obedience to Him. It was His commitment to stay the course as He faced the demands of the cross that held Him steady when His flesh recoiled from what lay ahead. He was committed to this supreme expression of God's love. As we have seen, commitment is the glue that helps us express love even when it is hard and difficult to do so.

My daughter, an elementary teacher, once asked her class to name their heroes. Most of the children chose the usual heroes. One little boy, however, chose Jesus. His choice, along with others, was posted on the classroom bulletin board. Billy Graham and Mother Teresa chose Jesus as their hero. We too can choose Jesus as our Hero and put Him on the bulletin board of our lives. We probably will not get any endorsement deals, but look at what our Hero did. He ended up changing the world by giving Himself in selfless humility to die on the cross. The world has never been the same.

Many people at the cross thought Jesus had lost, but instead He had won a battle that could not be won any other way. Think of the positive impact we can have in our relationships when we give up our rights to win or choose our own selfish ways. We just might change our home. We just might change our church. We just might help convince some people to become believers. As we choose to express love like our Hero, Jesus, we just might change our world. It's an excellent way to live.

## Further study, reflection, and discussion:

1. Use the Scriptures in this chapter for more detailed personal or group study.
2. What are some of the heroes popular in our culture? Who is your favorite?
3. Why do we find it difficult to be others-centered?
4. Why is it hard to "win" an argument with someone else?
5. Why do we find it hard to say "I'm sorry" in our relationships?
6. Identify some of the rejected people of society in your area and strategize how you can reach out to them.

15

# Don't Fake It

*Woe to you teachers of the law and Pharisees, you hypocrites! You shut the kingdom of heaven in men's faces. You yourselves do not enter, nor will you let those enter who are trying to* (Matthew 23:13).

Sophie, along with her husband and two children lived in a modest home in a bustling neighborhood of people much like them. Money was tight because of a strike the previous year at the factory where her husband, Mike, worked. Sophie was the lead singer in the worship band in their local church. Mike was the president of the local little league. Sophie became the league treasurer since she was good at handling finances.

At a meeting of the league officers, however, someone noticed the figures in the financial report did not accurately reflect some expenses. An audit and investigation revealed Sophie had used league money to buy clothing and jewelry for herself and her family.

The impact reverberated through their church and community. The media cataloged Sophie's deception and dishonesty for days. Mike had to quit his job at the factory. He was a marked man. Their children were taken to their grandparents to live because of the abuse at school. Their church was devastated, knowing they would be known in the community as Sophie's church. Sophie and Mike eventually repaid the money, but she was found guilty of embezzlement. Sadly, Sophie's story is repeated from time to time by others who profess to be Christians.

## The World Watches

Hypocrisy in church circles can be best described as sin dressed up in Christian clothing. We all have been outraged at the clergy scandals involving sexual abuse and misuse of money that have severely damaged the image of the church in recent years. Unfortunately, these are just the scandals emphasized by the media. When any believer lives a contradictory life, it has an enormous impact on those around them.

Whether we like it or not, unbelievers watch us. They hear what we say but they also watch what we do. Thankfully most of us have not made Sophie's mistake, but how we treat our family, the neighbors, and fellow workers leaves an impact.

A pastor was stopped at a red light in town when he noticed two drivers involved in shouting and horn honking. He was surprised when he realized one of the drivers attended the church where he was the pastor. It was not some terrible sin, but he wondered to himself how many others were watching.

Jesus gave a scathing rebuke to the Pharisees and teachers of the law in Matthew 23. Six times he called them hypocrites. He showed the impact of their hypocrisy in verse 13, "You shut the kingdom of heaven in men's faces. You yourselves do not enter, nor will you let those enter who are trying to."

He described them in graphic terms in verses 27-28,

*You are like whitewashed tombs, which look beautiful on the outside but on the inside are full of dead men's bones and everything unclean. In the same way, on the outside you appear to people as righteous but on the inside you are full of hypocrisy and wickedness.*

Jesus used His harshest words to expose their duplicity and wickedness. Troubled over the sinfulness of the Jews of His day, Jesus' reactions to it is described in Luke 19:41, "As he approached Jerusalem and saw the city, he wept over it." The wickedness and hypocrisy of His day was of deep, heart-wrenching concern to Jesus. He has the same concern for us today.

Jesus talked about the whitewashed tombs of His time. Unfortunately, the Christian faith of some believers is like a thin veneer of wallpaper covering a bare and unfinished wall. It may look pretty on the outside but underneath are cracks, stains, and other unsightly marks. This is because some of us have not taken the time or made the effort to learn how God wants us to live. We live contradictory lives because of our ignorance. Others, like Sophie, know what the Bible teaches but fail to apply it in their lives. Churches that fail to teach biblical values must share in the blame as well. Perhaps those who call us hypocrites have a point.

Thomas Reeves stated,

Christianity in modern America is, in large part, innocuous. It tends to be easy, upbeat, convenient, and compatible. It does not require self-sacrifice, discipline, humility, an otherworldly outlook, a zeal for souls, a fear as well as love of God. There is little guilt and no punishment, and the payoff in heaven is virtually certain.

This type of spiritual atmosphere produces a shallow Christian life where hypocrisy is encouraged and the church forfeits its moral obligation to offer an alternative.

All of us agree that no one likes a fake, especially a religious one. When a person's actions do not match their words it makes us wonder, "What are they up to?" Eventually Sophie's deception was discovered. It is easy, however, to point fingers at other Christians who get media attention for their misdeeds. As believers we can ask ourselves, "How concerned am I about hypocrisy in my life?" This is tremendously important for God's kingdom because being real and genuine will pay enormous dividends in this life and for eternity.

## God Is Watching

Sometimes we try, like Sophie, to hide our hypocrisy from others. We may be successful for a time, but we cannot hide it from God. Mark 12:13-17 describes the Pharisees and Herodians coming to Jesus with a question. They ask him about paying taxes to Caesar. They were not really interested in taxes; their real purpose was to catch Jesus in His words. Verse 15 tells us, "Jesus knew their hypocrisy."

Jesus quoted from Isaiah in Mark 7:6 where he described hypocrites' actions, "These people honor me with their lips, but their hearts are far from me." While others may not know who we really are, we may be sure Jesus knows what is in our hearts.

Paul addresses this problem in Romans 12:9, "Love must be sincere." The word used for *sincere* means not hypocritical. The word for hypocrite is taken from a term describing Greek actors who used masks to play the role of several different characters. Even today we use the phrase to wear a mask to disguise what we are on the inside by hiding our true feeling and intentions.

That was Sophie's mistake. She played a role that was not real. As believers we do not want to wear masks or play fictitious roles. Living in love toward God and others means we can live transparent lives that are real and genuine.

Jesus focused attention on the hypocrisy of the Pharisees. What would He say and do if He came to our town, to our church, or to our house? If the polls are correct, some Christians have a problem that needs to be addressed. None of us will be perfect in this life, but we do not want to become like Sophie either. Hiding our sins only makes matters worse. People are watching us. More importantly, God is watching. How soon we apologize and ask for forgiveness lets people know we are trying to be open and transparent.

We need to be honest with ourselves. We need to be real and genuine. Our lives can make a difference right where we live. As we make an earnest effort to live in love toward God and others, we can demonstrate to our world that not all Christians are hypocrites. Too much is at stake as we seek to excel in our world.

## Further study, reflection, and discussion:

1. Use the Scriptures in this chapter for more detailed personal or group study.
2. Why do you think non-believers view believers as hypocritical?
3. What behavior in your life could be seen as hypocritical?
4. What changes do you need to make to correct this?

# 16

# Love Him Back!

*But be very careful to keep the commandment and the law that Moses the servant of the Lord gave to you: to love the Lord your God, to walk in all his ways, to obey his commands, to hold fast to him and serve him with all your heart and soul* (Joshua 22:5).

One of the joys of being a grandparent is of course the grandchildren themselves. There are four girls and three boys in our clan. The boys enjoy sports along with rough and tumble play. When they were younger the girls did not enjoy such things but preferred playing with dolls and the like. It was amusing to watch them play mother with their almost lifelike dolls. Their moms had a close-up view of their own actions parodied in their girls.

The girls fed, washed, and played with them until the buttons on the clothes fell off and the artificial hair came out. The dolls were hugged and hugged and often were found in the girls arms when they fell asleep at night. The irony of it all was, as much attention as our granddaughters lavished on them, the dolls could never respond.

Though we are not dolls, God must feel the same way about us at times. He loves us, but at times we fail to love Him back. Dolls cannot do that, but we can. Sometimes we refrain from showing Him love out of ignorance, and at other times it is done through willful choice. If the foundation of love is commitment, then we can measure our commitment to God by how well our love is expressed back to Him. It is important for believers to know how to do this.

How much do we think about God in our daily lives? Is He just a Sunday morning experience when we conveniently have time or a first aid kit when trouble comes? If we are going to love God back, He must occupy first place in our lives. Our lives must truly center on Him.

## Trust God

Trust is a vital part of any relationship. We trust the bank to take care of our money. We trust the doctor to help us get healthy. We try to find a mechanic we can trust to repair our car. When trust is not fulfilled, relationships fail. We change banks, doctors, and mechanics.

Some of us are reluctant to put our trust and faith in God. Usually it is because we think God has failed us in some way. We don't realize that God is not like a soda machine where we put in our money and select whatever flavor we want.

Let's look at God's record. He made a covenant agreement with Noah and kept it. He made a covenant with Abraham and kept it. He made a covenant with the nation of Israel and has kept it. He promised to send the Messiah and sent Jesus to die on the cross for our sins.

The Bible is filled with God's promises to us. 2 Corinthians 1:20-22 reminds us, "For no matter how many promises God has made, they are 'Yes' in Christ. And so through him the 'Amen' is spoken in us to the glory of God. Now it is God who makes both us and you stand firm in Christ. He anointed us, set his seal of ownership on us, and put his Spirit in our hearts as a deposit, guaranteeing what is to come." What God has done for us in Christ is the ultimate assurance that He honors His promises. The Holy Spirit that God has placed in our hearts is the seal to this promise.

There is a great passage in Proverbs 3:5-6 that encourages us to put our trust in God. It states, "Trust in the Lord with all your heart and lean not on your own understanding; in all your ways acknowledge him, and he will make your paths straight." Notice the emphasis on "all your heart" and "all your ways." Many of us have embraced this as a life verse. What a statement of trust and faith expressing love back to God! This echoes what we learned from Deuteronomy 6:5 about loving God with all our heart, soul, and mind.

## Worship God

One of the most important things to do in marriage is to say "I love you" often. When we fail to do this often enough, our spouse begins to wonder if something is wrong. It is important to do this in our relationship with God as well. We do not want to take Him for granted either. Worship is a wonderful way to love Him back. Reading the Psalms gives us many examples.

Note the joyful excitement in Psalm 100, "Shout for joy to the Lord, all the earth. Worship the Lord with gladness; come before him with joyful songs. Know that the Lord is God. It is he who has made us, and we are his; we are his people, the sheep of his pasture. Enter his gates with thanksgiving and his courts with praise; give thanks to him and praise his name. For the Lord is good and his love endures forever; his faithfulness continues through all generations." Notice how exuberant and expressive this Psalm is. It teaches us we can find passion and intimacy with God in worship.

As we think about the wonder of belonging to the great Creator God, when we consider His great salvation in Christ, when we remember His provisions in so many ways, and we dwell on His goodness, love, and faithfulness, we are encouraged to "shout for joy to the Lord."

It is unfortunate that some of us have learned to be prim, proper, and restrained in worship. As we think about all the love God has given us, it is hard not to let our emotions soar in volumes of praise as the psalmist encourages us to do. Love will get us involved and excited about worshipping God. We can exclaim without fear or shame, "God, I love you!" We do not even need to be in a church service to do this. We can do it often, almost anywhere!

## Communicate with God

Communication is a key factor in expressing our love to God. If it is vital to the success of our marriage and family, it is also vital to the success of our relationship with God. In communicating with God there are three activities that are important: prayer, Bible study, and meditation.

Prayer is not complicated. It is talking to God the same way we would hold a conversation with a close friend. Paul stated in Colossians 4:2, "Devote yourselves to prayer, being watchful and thankful." He repeated his admonition in 1 Thessalonians 5:17. "Pray continually." We can talk to God often. He is waiting to hear from us.

Reading and studying the Bible is listening to God. Psalm 1:1-2 reminds us, "Blessed is the man who does not walk in the counsel of the wicked or stand in the way of sinners or sit in the seat of mockers. But his delight is in the law of the Lord, and on his law he meditates day and night." Remember the "hungry baby" metaphor in 1 Peter 2:2, "Like newborn babies, crave spiritual milk." Psalm 119:48 declares, "I reach out my hands for your commandments, which I love, and I meditate on your decrees." We can read it every day. God has much to say to us.

When we fail to give enough attention to what our spouse says to us, problems inevitably develop. Not long ago I brought the wrong item home from the grocery store because I hadn't listened carefully enough to my wife. Meditation is thinking deeply about God and what He says to us. When we meditate, we listen carefully to what God has said. This is how we internalize God's truths. It helps us give more attention to what God has said. It helps us learn His principles of moral excellence.

Doing these three things on a regular daily basis is vital if we want to have meaningful communication with God. We can find a time that fits our life and work schedule. When we miss a day for whatever reason, we can get back on track the next day.

## Obey God

Most of us have gotten lost going to some destination? Maybe the directions were wrong or we failed to look at the map. Even the GPS may have been programmed incorrectly. We never have to fear losing our way when we follow Jesus. He gave us clear directions in John 14:15, "If you love me, you will obey what I command." We can measure our commitment to love God by living in obedience to His commands.

Obedience is not because we are fearful of judgment, but because we have made a heart, soul, and mind commitment to do so. If we are going to love God back by obeying His commands, then we must take the time to learn and apply God's directions for living. That is the purpose of the Guide Book, the Bible.

One of Jesus' commands tells us in John 15:12, "My command is this: Love each other as I have loved you." John the Apostle wrote in 1 John 3:16-18, "This is how we know what love is: Jesus Christ laid down his life for us. And we ought to lay down our lives for our brothers. If anyone has material possessions and sees his brother in need but has no pity on him, how can the love of God be in him?" These verses show the clear connection between love of God and love of neighbor. They cannot be separated.

Our relationships with others are central in expressing love back to God. This can be challenging since some people are not easy to love, but it is what we are called to do if we want to seek the "high way." If we are honest with ourselves, all of us have bad hair days when we are not easy to love. It is wonderful when others choose to love us anyway.

God has loved us and loved us. He has shown in many ways that He desires to have a close relationship with each of us. We are not dolls who cannot respond. We can choose to express our love to God. We can love Him back as we trust Him with our all. We can love Him back as we express our joyful worship to Him. We can love God back as we communicate with Him in prayer. We can love God back as we read, study, and meditate on His Word. We can love Him back as we choose to live in obedience to His commands. We can love Him back as we love those around us. It's is how to live in excellence in our world.

## Further study, reflection, and discussion:

1. Use the Scriptures in this chapter for more detailed personal or group study.
2. What areas of your life are you keeping for yourself and away from God?
3. Why is it important for us to take time in our prayer lives to praise God for who He is?
4. Why are some believers reluctant to be expressive in their worship of God?
5. Why are mercy and forgiveness so important in our relationships?

17

# Fly Like the Geese

You don't choose your family. They are God's gift to you, as you are to them. —*Desmond Tutu*

Seagulls offer a study in group violence. The idea of sharing does not seem to exist with them. They are bold and brazen, flying in your face to demand a scrap of food. Fiercely competitive and jealous, they will attack and kill another gull that is somehow different.

Wild geese, on the other hand, offer an example of group cooperation. Everyone has seen their V-formation silhouetted in the sky. The point position is the most difficult, so leaders trade positions every few minutes. Young, weak, and older birds fly in the two rear sections. They fly as a family. They also have a built-in guidance system to get them to their destination.[1]

## Families in Trouble

What kind of family do we want? Do we want to be like seagulls or wild geese? One lives for itself; the other lives for the group. Because of the rejection of traditional values, our culture is developing a lot of seagull families.

The results of the secular progressive effort to rebuild marriage their way are not encouraging. Earlier it was noted that the 2010 census data indicates only 48% of households in our country consist of a traditional husband and wife. Divorce, blended families, and family dysfunction appear to be the rule not the exception. Some people in our country even think that marriage is obsolete. Many people are deciding just to live together. Many others are working to redefine marriage legally and break the biblical pattern of one man and one woman.

Unfortunately, this is a critical area where some Christians are also living by the world's rules, not God's pattern taught in the Bible. Statistics reveal divorce is common among Christians. The battle for our minds is also a battle for the family.

Since the home is the foundation of society, it is ground zero where it is vital for biblical love to be practiced. The teaching and training of our families according to God's kingdom principles is a critical task of the church in our culture.

It is not just the individual believer who must learn how to swim against the swift, strong current of our secular culture. Families are in the same current together. We need all the help the church can give us to swim together in rhythm as a family.

Kenneth Chafin has stated,

> There is no way to build a happy, effective family on an inadequate relationship between a husband and wife. It is like building a house "upon the sand" and the pressures and problems which would be handled easily by other families will cause this one to shake and possibly even crumble."[2]

We have seen earlier that love is to be the foundational principle in all our relationships. Unfortunately, the popular concept of love in our culture does not prepare us well for marriage. What happens in many relationships can be described with the following story.

Mack and Linda began like many couples. After a few dates they fell in love and after a time decided to get married. Things went well for a few months. Mack was caught up in his job and sports. Linda was working and going to college several nights a week to finish her degree. They were living busy lives. The feelings that drew them together began to fade. They began to think perhaps they had made a mistake.

Studies show the feelings that begin a marriage decline up to 80% after eighteen months to two years. Many couples are not prepared for this, and the marriage for some ends in anger, frustration, and disappointment. Some who stay together live in a guarded truce between arguments with an underlying sense of unhappiness and regret.

## Turning Our Families Around

As we have seen previously, this is where the commitment to act in loving ways has to be made. It is not about "what's in it for me." It is not about winning. It is about choosing to stop the arguing and bickering and making a decision to act in loving ways toward one's spouse. Stephen and Alex Kendrick's movie *Fireproof*, along with their book, *The Love Dare*, shows how this can work.

Chafin gives three basic areas in a marriage where love must find practical expression.[3] The first is accommodation to each other in love and respect. The normal differences between male and female, different personalities, along with different family backgrounds means each partner must be willing to change and adjust to these differences. Mack and Linda brought different personal expectations into their marriage. Mack liked his sports and Linda was determined to finish her degree.

Second, he mentions communication. Couples need to talk and talk and talk some more, verbalizing and expressing their thoughts and feelings. The other side of communication is listening to one another, hearing not just one another's words but each other's heart. Mack and Linda were too busy to communicate since each went their separate busy ways.

The last point he calls "from me to us." This is the realization that a couple is just that—a separate, unique twosome plus the addition of children. There must be a permanent commitment to one's spouse and children. Previous relationships of family and friends need to be adjusted to account for this. Mack and Linda were still focused on the "me, my, and mine" of personal concerns and desires.

## Family Roles

It is also important to study Ephesians 5:22-6:4, a passage often misunderstood and misapplied. The first section has captured the most attention where Paul states in vs. 22, "Wives, submit to your husbands, as to the Lord." Sadly, some men, thinking like the seagull, seem to stop here, thinking if our wives would just do this, marriage would be wonderful. We fail to ask one simple question, "Why would my wife do this?"

Paul answers this question in vs. 25, "Husbands, love your wives, just as Christ loved the church and gave himself for her." The husband cannot act like a king of the castle. Since a wife's submission is to be "as to the Lord," it cannot be demanded but it must be voluntary and under the same conditions established by Christ. Only when a wife is made to feel safe, secure, valued, and respected can she do this.

Paul is clear about the husband's position at the point of the V-formation of the family. The husband is to establish a family environment where the wife and the children are loved and protected. Being the head of the home does not mean the husband can be a selfish seagull. Rather, he brings his unique talents and abilities to his family using them for the greater good of all.

Modeled on Christ's example, the selfless giving of the husband creates a level of trust where the wife and children will feel confident enough to follow. They know they are valued because he tells them and shows them he loves them. He makes time for them in spite of outside pressures. They know the husband will do his best to provide for them because he works hard and honestly. They know that he has their best interests at heart because he asks and values their opinions. This is how a husband earns the respect of his wife and the obedience of his children. He is answerable to God for how well he leads in this vital area.

Wives are to express their love by submitting to the husband and giving him the respect his efforts deserve. This does not mean the wife is the family doormat. It means she willingly joins hands with her husband to build a home where selfless love is the model for the children. She will do her part to support him; even taking a turn at the point of the V should that be required.

She cannot be a seagull either, putting her own desires above her family. She also uses her unique talents and abilities for the greater good of her family. She is answerable to God for how well she does this. This goes a long way toward helping a couple build together the right environment of cooperation in the home.

Some of us accept the biblical order of the family without question, while others may be confused about our roles. To understand the function of the family, it is worth studying the nature of God. The Bible teaches that God is three-in-one: Father, Son, and Holy Spirit. This is called the Trinity. The Son is eternally generated by the Father. The Holy Spirit is eternally generated by the Father and the Son. Simply put, while being co-equal, there is perfect love and cooperation in the Trinity. This is where God took His model for the family.

## Helping Children Learn to Fly

Children are masters at the tactic of divide and conquer. When wives and husbands model cooperation and agree on family values, children cannot rule the roost. They are precious treasures given by God. Love respects the unique qualities of each child and provides the guidance they need for them to develop godly character and discover God's will for their lives.

Children are admonished in Ephesians 6:1, "obey your parents in the Lord for this is right." This is how children can express love to their parents. Given the right home environment of unconditional love, most children will do this with a minimum application of tough love. Children will be answerable to God for how they respond to us. They learn not to be seagulls by watching and obeying us.

Paul gives a warning to fathers (and mothers) in Ephesians 6:4, "Do not exasperate your children." Paul's meaning is for us to avoid harsh, unreasonable punishment that leaves children feeling trapped and confused.

Eric Buehrer gives three questions to ask ourselves that will help us have a positive influence on our children.[4] First, "What do I teach my child?" This is where learning God's kingdom principles is so important. We cannot teach our children what we ourselves do not know.

Next, we are to ask, "How can I model it for my child?" This is how children learn to fly like the geese. Children are remarkable at noticing the difference between what we say and what we do.

Lastly, we need to ask, "What can I encourage in my child?" Encouragement is like fertilizer to plants causing them to grow and become productive. It makes children feel confident and supported as they grow toward adulthood. Correction should produce a positive not a negative atmosphere. Even when parents make mistakes, and we all do, children are remarkably resilient and forgiving if they know they are loved unconditionally.

Mack and Linda decided to seek counseling together, something they should have done before they were married. They were referred to a local Christian counseling center where it did not take long for them to learn they were both living like seagulls. Making a renewed commitment to their marriage, they decided to make some changes.

Mack cut back on his sports. Linda reduced her college course load. They made plans to spend at least one night a week as a special date night just for the two of them. After awhile they noticed the glow returning to their relationship, only this time it was even stronger. They had begun to fly together as a family.

This chapter does not give a detailed list of answers to family issues. It is intended to give us a basic attitude to help us learn how to function as a family. Seagull families do not function well. Many of them disintegrate and the children inherit the results.

Remember, when our families fly like the wild geese, and we are living in love toward each other, we are modeling the very nature of God. This makes the way our families live together special and important. We need to take time to learn how love can work in our families. It is how we can excel as a family in our world.

[1]Michael P. Green, Ed., *Illustrations for Biblical Preaching* (Grand Rapids: Baker Book House, 1989), 145-146.
[2]Kenneth Chafin, *Is There a Family in the House?* (Minneapolis, MN.: World Wide Publications, 1978), 50.
[3]Ibid., 32-37.
[4]Eric Buehrer, *Charting Your Family's Course* (Wheaton, IL.: Victor Books, 1994), 23.

## Further study, reflection, and discussion:

1. What do you use to guide you in the way your family functions and makes decisions?
2. Use Ephesians 5:22-6:4 and Colossians 3:18-21 for more detailed personal or group study.
3. Watch the movie *Fireproof*.
4. How can a husband and wife work together to develop an atmosphere where children will learn biblical values?

18

# Built Up To Grow!

*Now you are the body of Christ, and each one of you is a part of it*
(1 Corinthians 12:27).

Mary was a teenager sprouting her wings to adulthood. She was not a re-
bellious, wild teen bent on enjoying life without restraint. However, she made
an unwise life-changing decision—she became pregnant. Mary and her family
attended Westside Community Chapel. It did not take long for the news to
spread. Soon Mary heard some unkind remarks from several church members
about her behavior. She was crushed and angry that fellow Christians could be
this judgmental and condemning, so she stopped attending church.

Mary's story illustrates the cliché that "Christians shoot their wounded."
When we should bring healing to the hurting and help to the sinner, the Bible is
used to condemn and beat them down further instead. It is unfortunate to hear
Christians speak in such condemning tones about those among us who fail at
times to live by Christian values. Could this be one of the reasons the church
has such limited support and respect in our culture?

## Correct Belief

There is a challenging story for us in Matthew 12:1-8. Jesus and His disciples were going through the grain fields on the Sabbath. When they picked
some of the grain and ate it, the Pharisees condemned them for breaking the
rules of the Sabbath. Jesus' answer reminded them that David and his men had
eaten the consecrated bread from the temple. He then quoted from Hosea 6:6,
"I desire mercy and not sacrifice." The focus of the Pharisees on the minute details of their interpretations of the Law was off target. Jesus taught that there
are principles more important than a strict adherence to the laws of sacrifice.
The Pharisees had omitted mercy.

What we believe is important, but how we treat people is more important
than strict adherence to doctrine. When you get right down to it, belief in the
right doctrine is not correct if the expression of God's love is ignored. Our faith
is like a jigsaw puzzle with some pieces missing.

Jesus understood this when He condemned the Pharisees in Matthew 23:23

declaring, "Woe to you, teachers of the law and Pharisees, you hypocrites! You give a tenth of your spices—mint, dill and cumin. But you have neglected the more important matters of the law – justice, mercy and faithfulness. You should have practiced the latter, without neglecting the former." Jesus again showed how the Pharisees and teachers of the law made the mistake of letting adherence to their rigid theology blind them to the more important aspects of serving God—justice, mercy and faithfulness.

We may condemn the Pharisees for their shortsighted legalism, but the truth is some Christians have been just as guilty as the Pharisees. Mary's experience reminds us that our allegiance to what we believe can blind us to love, mercy, and forgiveness. We can be faithful paying our tithes, but if we forget the church is to be a hospital for healing and not a courthouse of judgment, we make the same mistake as the Pharisees. Our goal in the church is to restore, heal, and build up one another.

## Whose Church Is It?

First Church was in turmoil over the pastor's preaching on controversial topics. Some members were supportive, but a majority was opposed so the tension increased. Finally, the pastor resigned in frustration, taking his supporters with him to start a new church in a local school. A once united group of believers were fractured. Some stopped going to either church.

First Church is an example of what has happened countless times past and present. One group leaves and meets elsewhere with each side convinced the other is wrong and heretical. Communication and fellowship ties are severed. Think of the picture this presents to others. Two groups of believers, who no longer talk to each other begin meeting in separate places, each group continuing to expect God to bless them.

What message are we sending our community? Instead of demonstrating the love of Christ, we express our flawed attitudes and lack of love toward others. Too many Christians have not learned to disagree without being disagreeable. This error is often made because we fail to separate our egos from our ideas. Part of the answer to where the church has gone wrong lies in how we view ourselves as God's church. The church is not just another human organization to be shaped according to each member's own ideas and attitudes.

Paul gave us a biblical view that needs re-emphasis today. He stated in Ephesians 2:19-22,

> *Consequently, you are no longer foreigners and aliens, but fellow citizens with God's people and members of God's household, built on the foundation of the apostles and prophets, with Christ Jesus himself as*

*the chief cornerstone. In him the whole building is joined together and rises to become a holy temple in the Lord. And in him you too are being built together to become a dwelling in which God lives by his Spirit.*

The church is to be first and foremost "a dwelling in which God lives by his Spirit" where we see ourselves as "fellow citizens" and "members of God's household." This is far from being a social club with a narrow vision and membership.

Though we can speak of a local church as our church, it is not really ours. Christ is the Head of the church. The Holy Spirit dwells there among His people. He has graciously invited us to be a part of this fellowship. As we learn to think of the church in biblical terms, it will have an enormous impact on how we conduct ourselves collectively as believers.

## The Role of Leadership

Leadership plays a vital role in this. Ephesians 4:11-13 gives one of the main functions of leadership in the church.

*It was he who gave some to be apostles, some to be prophets, some to be evangelists, and some to be pastors and teachers, to prepare God's people for works of service, so that the body of Christ may be built up until we all reach unity in the faith and in the knowledge of the Son of God and become mature, attaining to the whole measure of the fullness of Christ.*

Don attended a state university to study to become a lawyer. His freshman year he was confronted with professors and fellow students who did not share the Christian beliefs he had learned as a child. His course in Introduction to Philosophy was taught by an atheist. Don became confused and began having doubts about what he had been taught.

His parents were concerned that he did not want to attend church when he came home for a weekend. They had no answers for the questions he asked. Conversations turned into arguments. Sadly, this family's dilemma has been repeated countless times as parents helplessly watched their children turn away from God under the influence of a secular education.

We are in a battle for the hearts and minds of those who want to follow Christ. The teaching and training of believers to live in love toward God and others is a fundamental task of church leadership if we are to win this battle. It is vital that we become "built up, reach unity. . .and become mature." If we are just caught up in contemporary methods and programs but fail to provide the biblical knowledge that believers need to combat the belief systems of our world, we will fall short in fulfilling a basic command of God's Word.

It is a task that must be carefully planned if believers are to become mature and the church is to fulfill its mission. The believer's Guide Book, the Bible, should be used so that people can read and study what the Scriptures actually teach. Sending believers unprepared into a secular, godless world is a prescription for personal and collective spiritual failure.

Peter spoke also to church leaders in 1 Peter 5:2-3,

*Be shepherds of God's flock that is under your care, serving as over- seers—not because you must, but because you are willing, as God wants you to be; not greedy for money, but eager to serve; not lording it over those entrusted to you, but being examples to the flock.*

Just because some of us are leaders does not mean the church is ours to possess. God calls us to be under shepherds and servant leaders not CEOs. It is God's flock and church leaders are *His* overseers. One day God will ask us to give an accounting of our stewardship. The local church should not revolve around a person but around kingdom principles. Living in love toward God and others is the only way to provide a stable foundation for leadership in the church.

When leadership does its job of preparing believers, there will be a cascading result. Paul gave a brief but powerful summary in Ephesians 4:14-16,

*Then we will no longer be infants, tossed back and forth by the waves, and blown here and there by every wind of teaching and by the cunning and craftiness of men in their deceitful scheming, instead, speaking the truth in love, we will in all things grow up into him who is the Head, that is, Christ. From him the whole body, joined and held together by every supporting ligament, grows and builds itself up in love, as each part does its work.*

Unity, stability, and growth are hallmarks of a healthy church. Every believer is important in achieving these goals. Building one another up in love plays a central role. For example, when he was a teenager, Don's youth group focused on entertainment and fellowship not biblical principles for living a godly life. This was also lacking when First Church split into two separate congregations. They were so focused on correct theology that they neglected their relationships as followers of Christ. As believers, we need to ask ourselves if we are helping or hindering the process of building up fellow Christians. Is our church expressing flawed sinful attitudes, or is it becoming what God intended it to be?

# Serving in Love

Peter gave us more insight in 1 Peter 4:8-11,

*Above all, love each other deeply, because love covers a multitude of sins. Offer hospitality to one another without grumbling. Each one should use whatever gift he has received to serve others, faithfully administering God's grace in its various forms. If anyone speaks, he should do it as one speaking the very words of God. If anyone serves, he should do it with the strength God provides, so that in all things God may be praised through Jesus Christ.*

As believers we need to be released to use our God-given gifts to serve in a needy world. Our gifts are from God and are to be expressions of His love. They are not ours to possess selfishly but are to be used in faithful service to others.

Peter gives us a good question to ask, "Are my speech and actions going to bring praise to God from others who are watching?" If we are living in love toward God and others, we will find the right answer.

The church, as it should, does many good things around the world. However, it is worth noting what Paul said in 1 Corinthians 13:1-3,

*If I speak in the tongues of men and of angels, but have not love, I am only a resounding gong or a clanging cymbal. If I have the gift of prophecy and can fathom all mysteries and all knowledge, and if I have a faith that can move mountains, but have not love, I am nothing. If I give all I possess to the poor and surrender my body to the flames, but have not love, I gain nothing.*

It is not about our gifts and abilities, as fine as these are. The most important thing we can do as members and leaders of a church is to live in love toward God and others. This will undergird and strengthen what we do by gaining the respect of those watching. Keep in mind the church is not filled with perfect people. After all, you and I are a part of it too. All believers are flawed humans who have a desire to follow Christ. Paul's letters to the churches of his day let us know that life in the church can get messy and complicated at times.

Mary was crushed at first by the judgment of her fellow believers until a couple from her church reached out to her and her family. Mary received the support and love she needed to get past her tragic mistake. It took awhile, but Mary eventually became a confident adult who served in her church. (By the way, as we might expect, the baby was beautiful.)

A friend invited Don to a Christian campus group where he was able to talk to people who helped him deal with the questions raised by secular professors. It was not long until Don recommitted his life to serve Christ.

If we as the church are going to impact the world, imitating Jesus' attitude and behavior must be the first order of business. Next to the family, the church is to be a model for the practice of biblical love. Believing correct doctrines is not enough. Adopting contemporary methods is not enough.

Serving with love, mercy, and justice is what Jesus taught and practiced. There are some like Mary and others like Don who need us. Church leaders must provide believers with the teaching and training needed to live in a secular world. It is how we can change the perception of the church as legalistic, judgmental, and hypocritical. It is a vital way that we, the church, need to excel in our world.

## Further study, reflection, and discussion:

1. Use the Scriptures in this chapter for more detailed personal or group study.
2. Why do you think more people not come to your church?
3. Do you expect your fellow believers to forgive you when you do something wrong? Why?
4. Have you ever been wounded by other Christians? How did you react? How should you react?
5. How do you react when your ideas are not accepted by your church group?

19

# Blimps and Dump Trucks?

Preach the gospel at all times. If necessary, use words. —*St. Francis of Assisi*

A number of years ago, Joseph Bayly wrote a book entitled, *The Gospel Blimp.*[1] It is a delightful satire about a group of people who tried to reach their town with the gospel using a blimp. It details their humorous but misguided attempts that often antagonized people instead of winning them to Christ. Gospel tracts dumped from the blimp littered peoples' lawns, stopped up their gutters, and even caught fire in a barbecue grill.

The story ends with one of the original members of the blimp team, George, dropping out and winning his neighbor to Christ by helping him in a time of crisis. Bayly craftily uses humor to show the most effective way to reach people for the Lord is to demonstrate God's love to them as practical, caring friends and neighbors.

## Be a Friend

If we want to express love toward others and be obedient to the teachings of Christ, what Jesus said in Matthew 28:19-20 gives us clear direction in a critical area.

*Therefore go and make disciples of all nations, baptizing them in the name of the Father and of the Son and of the Holy Spirit, and teaching them to obey everything I have commanded you.*

How we live each day impacts those around us and can open or close doors to sharing Christ with them.

Friendship evangelism has been used to describe the most productive way to reach others for Christ. This is the opposite of dump truck evangelism where the gospel is dumped on people without regard to their needs or where they are spiritually. Some people have distributed gospel tracts on a public street or beach only to find most of them tossed in a nearby trash can or littering the ground. While God does at times use our flawed, stumbling efforts to win others to Christ, He does so in spite of our mistakes. As Bayly's book demonstrates, this can waste time and money that can be used more effectively in other ways.

Ephesians 4:12 emphasizes the preparing or training of God's people for works of service. When we seek to win unbelievers to Christ, this is critical. The vast majority of people who accept Christ do so outside a church, usually in their contacts with a believer. This means there are countless opportunities to offer people genuine, caring friendship.

This does not mean friendship is to be used by us as a tool of gospel scalp hunters ready to pounce on needy sinners. Remember, love needs to be sincere. It simply means an atmosphere can be created by the way we live that will provide the Holy Spirit with the opportunities to work in peoples' lives and draw them to Christ. He may or may not actually use us to lead them to Christ, but we can be an important part of the process by laying a foundation.

How can we do this? Jesus indicated in Matthew 10:42 that giving something as small as a cup of cold water is important. We do not have to try and make a big impression with some grandiose display. We can show we genuinely care by following through with an appropriate act of friendship. The couple in Bayly's story helped out when the neighbor's wife was in the hospital. They also took time to show them real friendship. Our lives too will count for Christ as we show our love for others by offering genuine friendship and hospitality to those near us.

As we offer caring friendship, we will have the opportunity to share what Christ means to us and how He has changed us. We do not have to be argumentative, we just tell our story. What God has done for us is a powerful witness. D. T. Niles described sharing the gospel this way, "Christianity is one beggar telling another beggar where he found bread." We cannot save them. Only the Holy Spirit can do that. We can pray for the Holy Spirit to open their hearts and we can pray for guidance for what to say and do.

## How to Accept Christ

Along with telling our own story of salvation, we also can be ready to explain to those who are ready how to accept Christ. Many believers are afraid because they are not sure how to do this properly. It really is not all that difficult. We can be ready to share with them by highlighting the following verses in our Bible.

*Genesis 1:27 tells us, "God created man in his own image."* They started well, but the story of Adam and Eve in Genesis 3 indicates their disobedience to God's command brought sin into our lives. God's image in us has been marred as a result. The story of Christ tells us how God has dealt with the problem of evil that touches each of us.

*Romans 3:23, "For all have sinned and fall short of the glory of God."* This verse tells us that everyone has sinned in some way. There are no perfect people. Most of us like to think of ourselves as good people, and to a degree we are. The problem is that we measure our lives against others who are not as good. What we fail to realize is we are using the wrong ruler. This verse tells us that, though some of us have lived better lives than others, all of us fail to live up to God's glory. As was previously noted, none of us can swim to Bermuda or Hawaii.

*Romans 6:23 states, "For the wages of sin is death, but the gift of God is eternal life in Christ Jesus our Lord."* This verse has a dual message. A sinful life has consequences that can lead to an early grave and more importantly, death in eternity apart from God. Unfortunately, we are frequently reminded by the media of the tragic end to the lives of famous people because of poor choices.

The alternative to this dismal prospect is that God offers the gift of eternal life through Christ. A gift is bought by the giver, paying a price for the item. Christ's death on the cross has made the gift of eternal life possible. We can choose to accept or reject the gift God offers.

*Ephesians 2:8-9 tells us, "For it is by grace you have been saved, through faith—and this not from yourselves, it is the gift of God—not by works, so no one can boast."* Many people think God will let them into heaven if they live a good life. But how good do we have to be? Who decides? What is good enough?

Paul is writing to remind us that we cannot earn our salvation. It is given by God's grace or unmerited favor in response to our faith in Christ's death for us on the cross. Every time our family celebrates a grandchild's birthday, our gifts are eagerly opened without hesitation. We can receive God's gift of salvation the same way.

*Acts 3:19 says, "Repent, then, and turn to God, so that your sins may be wiped out, that times of refreshing may come from the Lord, and that he may send the Christ, who has been appointed for you—even Jesus."* Repentance from our sins is the message to emphasize.

When we are traveling and realize we are headed in the wrong direction, the voice on the GPS tells us, "At the next intersection make a u-turn." We solve the problem by turning around and heading in a new direction. Repentance means to change the direction of our lives by turning from our sins toward God and asking His forgiveness through Christ.

*John 1:12 gives a wonderful promise. "Yet to all who received him, to those who believed in his name, he gave the right to become children of God."* Our response is to believe God and receive what God offers in Christ.

If a local store gives away free gifts as a promotion, the line forms around the block. Some people camp out all night just to be first. God is offering us the free gift of eternal life in Christ. Just like the grandkids, all we have to do is reach out and take it. As we do this, as we open our hearts and lives in faith to God's offer, we become children of God.

*Revelation 3:20 provides an invitation. Jesus said, "Here I am! I stand at the door and knock. If anyone hears my voice and opens the door, I will go in and eat with him, and he with me."* We all like to get invitations to a party or get-together. We like to enjoy a good time with family and friends. It is a time to relax and let our hair down. Being together to laugh and share stories creates happy memories. It almost always involves good food. Eating a meal with someone in Bible times was a lot like that. It meant the inclusion of that person in one's life.

This verse says Jesus is knocking at the door of our hearts and lives. He is offering us a personal relationship that will be deeply satisfying and rewarding. We are encouraged to open the door. Christ says He will enter and begin the process of restoring God's image in us. We can invite those who open their hearts to Christ to our small group and to our church. We can continue to be their friend and mentor. This is what love does.

We don't need a blimp or a dump truck to spread the message of salvation in Christ. We can simply tell our own story of salvation. We can be a genuine friend to family, neighbors and fellow workers. When the time is right, we can use the Bible to show them the way to Christ. Our lives will count for God as we share His love with those we meet every day. It's an excellent way to live.

[1]Joseph Bayly, *The Gospel Blimp and other Modern Parables* (Colorado Springs, CO.: David C. cook, 2002).

## Further study, reflection, and discussion:

1. Use the Scriptures in this chapter for more detailed personal or group study.
2. Write down how you would explain the verses in this chapter to someone seeking Christ.
3. Take time to write down your personal testimony of salvation.
4. Why are we as believers the "only Bible some will ever read?"
5. How well do you get along with your family, neighbors, and fellow workers?
6. Why is it important for us to pray regularly for unsaved family members, neighbors, and fellow workers to be saved?
7. List some specific ways you can demonstrate love to your family, neighbors, and fellow workers.

20

# Is Love Color Blind?

*Be nice to whites, they need you to rediscover their humanity.*
—*Desmond Tutu*

It was a Sunday morning on September 15, 1963 when twenty-six children entered the basement of the 16th Street Baptist Church in Birmingham, Alabama. Shortly after 10:20 a.m. a bomb exploded killing four young black girls. It was a heinous crime that shocked the nation from its complacency and strongly influenced the passage of the Civil Rights Act of 1964.[1]

## An Embarrassing History

While other churches did not set the bomb in the 16th Street Baptist Church, some in the church had helped create a culture in which hate, not love was allowed to develop. The story of slavery in the United States is a cause of great embarrassment not only to our country but also to the church. While some churches protested vigorously against slavery, others were silent and some actually supported it. What has been done in the name of God is an unspeakably dark stain on the church.

Many of us today are unaware that Ephesians 6:5, "Slaves, obey your earthly masters" was used by some clergy and slave owners to tell slaves it was God's will they must obey their masters. Using Genesis 9:20-25, slaves were also told they were under God's curse because they were descendants of Ham, one of Noah's sons. Rather than giving people hope, they were told God had cursed them to an awful life of slavery.

The Klu Klux Klan has long used the Bible and the cross in their rituals, even burning crosses to intimidate blacks and others. Fear and intimidation is their message, not hope and love. These are just a few examples from our history that helped set the stage for what happened in Birmingham, Alabama.

Thankfully, slavery is no longer tolerated today, but the church in our country is still marked by congregations that are almost exclusively white, black, Hispanic, or some other ethnic group. Some churches have little interaction with other ethnic groups. We like to remain where we feel comfortable.

Racism in the church today is more subtle, but it is still there. It is not limited only to white people. It is easier to surround ourselves with people who look like us and act like us than to reach out to all people groups. We need to understand that racism can be something as simple as ignoring the invisible walls that separate us. Sin is not only what we do but also what we fail to do. It is imperative to confront the issues that divide us and ask, "How and why has this happened in the Body of Christ?" We need to know the answer to the question, "Is love color blind?"

Racism in the church is almost a forbidden topic to some. Some mistakenly believe there is little racism in our churches. But if we are going to discuss the implications of loving God and loving our neighbor as the foundation for our thought and behavior, then racism needs to be addressed on a personal and institutional level. God will hold us accountable if we do not do this. What will we say to Him when we all stand together in His presence one day?

## Dealing with the Past

As an Assembly of God minister, I am more aware of the history of my own denomination than others. An article in the *Pentecostal Evangel*, a weekly magazine published by the Assemblies of God, squarely confronted the history of racism that many in our denomination today did not know.

The modern Pentecostal movement began shortly after the start of the 20th century in a humble building on Azuza Street in Los Angeles in 1906. A revival began, led ironically by a black minister, William Seymour. This revival drew people from all over the United States and reverberated around the world. The meetings, which were interracial, continued until 1915. Today there are millions of Pentecostal believers in every country. That is the good news.

The Assemblies of God was started in 1913 as a result of the Azuza Street revival. Ministers and missionaries were ordained and commissioned. A black man from Chicago approached the officers of the Assemblies of God in 1917 for a missionary appointment to Liberia, Africa. He was informed that it was not God's will to send a "colored person" to do missions work in Africa.[2] Twenty two years later in 1939, a national policy was created that denied ordination to African-Americans. This policy persisted until it was overturned in 1962 when racism had become a national issue.[3] That is the bad news.

It is to the credit of the Assemblies of God that this dark cloud in its history has been dealt with openly. A meeting was held between the officials of the United Pentecostal Council of the Assemblies of God, a black denomination, and the Assemblies of God, a mostly white organization, on October 11-12, 2010 in Springfield, MO. The meeting proved to be a time of healing for a wound more than 90 years old.[4] The circle that began at Azuza Street is being closed.[5]

This story may make some of us uncomfortable, but the purpose is not to point fingers of blame at the past. It is to highlight the need today for us to rid ourselves of the attitudes and behaviors that contribute to the racial problems that persist in and outside the church.

## Clear Directions

The Bible gives us clear direction. Leviticus 19:33-34 declares,

*When an alien lives with you in your land, do not mistreat him. The alien living with you must be treated as one of your native-born. Love him as yourself, for you were aliens in Egypt. I am the Lord your God.*

The Book of Ruth tells the intriguing love story of a Moabite woman and a Jewish man who became the great grandparents of King David and ancestors of Jesus. The Moabites were longstanding enemies of the Jews. The New Testament speaks to the problems of racism as well. Many people read Jesus' parable of the Good Samaritan in Luke 10:30-37 and applaud the actions of the Samaritan who helped the man who was beaten, robbed, and left for dead.

What is missed today is the impact this had on those who heard Jesus tell the story. Jews and Samaritans hated each other. Jesus publicly chastised the Pharisees and teachers of the law by comparing their actions with a compassionate Samaritan. Those who heard Jesus clearly recognized the racial issues in this parable.

Paul was straightforward about the impact of salvation through Christ in Galatians 3:26-28,

*You are all sons of God through faith in Christ Jesus, for all of you who were baptized into Christ have clothed yourselves with Christ. There is neither Jew nor Greek, slave nor free, male nor female, for you are all one in Christ Jesus.*

He stated the same idea in Colossians 3:11, "Here there is no Greek or Jew, circumcised or uncircumcised, barbarian, Scythian, slave or free, but Christ is all, and is in all."

What makes these statements so impressive was Paul's own background as a Pharisee and the prevailing attitudes of the Roman world of that day. These words stand out like beacons in a dark, foggy night because they were addressed to cultures that were highly polarized around ethnic backgrounds and social standing. Unfortunately, divisions like this have persisted through history and are still with us today.

## The Answer

What is the answer to our question, "Is love color blind?" There need be no debate over this application of the principle of "love of neighbor". When Jesus died on the cross, His blood was shed for the sins of the whole world, not just one particular group of people who had the right skin color. If this life is to prepare us for heaven, then we have a lot of work to do. Thankfully, churches are not being bombed today, but there are many circles that still need closing.

First, we must repent as individuals and corporately as the church. Secondly, forgiveness needs to be extended to one another just as Jesus forgave those who crucified Him. Then, we must rise to the challenge of reconciliation in our day and time. This is what the United Pentecostal Council of the Assemblies of God and the Assemblies of God have done. May we reach out to one another in our communities and declare that love is indeed all encompassing regardless of race or color.

We have a lot of work to do. May our churches truly reflect the oneness for which Jesus prayed in John 17:21, "That all of them may be one, Father, just as you are in me and I am in you. May they also be in us so that the world may believe that you have sent me." Wouldn't this be an excellent way to live?

[1]wikipedia.org/wiki/16th Street Baptist Church Bombing. Accessed June 24, 2011.
[2]Scott Harrup, "A Larger Family." *Pentecostal Evangel* (January 16, 2011): 8.
[3]Ibid., 9.
[4]Ibid., 8.
[5]Ibid., 10.

## Further study, reflection, and discussion:

1. Use the Scriptures in this chapter for more detailed personal or group study.
2. How we help our church to confront racial problems in and outside the church?
3. What should we do when people use racial slurs or tell ethnic jokes?
4. Should the time of communion affect our attitude and actions toward people of other races?
5. How should giving to missions affect our prejudices toward others?
6. What steps can we take to unlearn prejudices we have developed toward others.

# 21

# Strong and Compassionate Love

*Jesus entered the temple and drove out all who were buying and selling
there. He overturned the tables of the money changers and the benches
of those selling doves* (Matthew 21:12).

Someone posted this comment on answers.yahoo.com. "Christians are
weak and they want to make the world as weak willed as they are by brain-
washing it and turning the planet into fools." This individual obviously has not
studied the Bible; however, this misguided idea has gained traction in our day.

Love is often portrayed as soft and easy. Meekness is thought of as weakness. Being a Christian is said to be weak and ignorant. Nothing could be further from the truth. Biblical love is neither soft, nor easy, nor weak. Whoever
said loving your enemy is easy has never tried. How easy is it to turn the other
cheek?

Living in God's love requires great strength and courage. Overcoming our
sinful tendencies takes dedication, persistence, and hard work. Parenting is a
challenge when a strong, compassionate love is required to change a child's behavior or to refuse their demands. It is not easy to say no and mean it over and
over again.

Programs dealing with people caught in the grip of substance abuse also
understand the need for a love that stands strong to help individuals withdraw
from drugs or alcohol. Alcoholics Anonymous uses the term *enabler* to describe those, who through ignorance or fear, enable people to remain in their
addictions by giving them what they want, not what they need. This application
of strong, compassionate love is not easy.

John was a lawyer with a thriving practice. He was married to Grace and
the father of two little girls. He and his family attended a local church. Life for
this young family changed dramatically when John began attending some meetings sponsored by a local religious cult. He began giving large sums of money
to the group and even left his wife and children. His wife, parents, and siblings
were desperate. After much prayer they made the difficult decision to hire a
group specializing in rescuing people from cults.

Fortunately, John's story had a happy ending. He was eventually depro-
grammed and set free. Thankfully, he was reunited with his wife and children.

It was far from easy and took a tremendous toll on his loved ones. It was strong, yet compassionate love that gave them the persistence needed to deal with an extremely difficult problem.

## God's Discipline

The writer of the book of Hebrews tells us that God at times uses this kind of love with us. Proverbs 3:11-12 is quoted in Hebrews 12:5-6, "My son, do not make light of the Lord's discipline, and do not lose heart when he rebukes you, because the Lord disciplines those he loves and he punishes everyone he accepts as a son." Verse 10 goes on to say, "God disciplines us for our own good, that we may share in his holiness." The way God treats us as sons and daughters gives us a model for strong, compassionate love. Like God, our love will choose to act in the best interests of others. This may not be what the person wants or expects, but it is needed for their good or the good of others.

Love with strength has a goal in mind that goes beyond a person's immediate desires. It is not to be vindictive or to inflict punishment. It is good to tell our children they need to eat their vegetables. However, parental persistence is needed, not punishment.

Some, unfortunately, have used this kind of love unwisely and have done more harm than good. A sledge hammer does not work too well to repair a car that doesn't start. It may just be out of gas or need a fuse. As we model God's love, we need to be firm but temper our actions with compassion and wisdom. The goal is one of redemption and restoration. We are reminded again of Paul's advice in Ephesians 5:15 of how important it is to "speak the truth in love."

## Love Lets Us Choose

Jesus gave us several examples of strong, compassionate love. One interesting story is found in Matthew 19:16-22 of the rich young man who asked Jesus the question, "Teacher, what good thing must I do to get eternal life?" Jesus answered him, "If you want to be perfect, go, sell your possessions and give to the poor, and you will have treasure in heaven. Then come, follow me." The young man on hearing this "went away sad, because he had great wealth." Jesus refused to tell him what was comfortable. Instead, He showed him the major hindrance in his life to following God. It is important to note also that Jesus did not run after the young man, begging him to change. He allowed him to experience the results of his own free choices

Jesus used this approach with both Judas and Peter when they celebrated the Passover together shortly before the crucifixion. Judas betrayed Him and Peter denied Him three times. Again, Jesus allowed them to make their choices.

Peter later repented while tragically Judas chose to hang himself. Jesus acted this way because He realized that change must come from the inside. We all must make the decision to change for ourselves. Strong, compassionate love presents us with the opportunity to decide.

## Confronting Sin

Most of us do not like confrontation and for a good reason. It is unpleasant and creates issues we would rather avoid. Jesus showed us, however, there are times love must be strong enough to confront sinful behavior, especially when it adversely affects others. The Scripture at the beginning of this chapter, Matthew 21:12, tells the story of Jesus when He drove the money changers and those selling animals for sacrifice from the temple.

These people were cheating those who came to the temple to offer sacrifices and pay the temple tax. Jesus boldly confronted those involved by physically driving them from the temple area. He also had harsh, stinging criticism for the teachers of the law and the Pharisees in Matthew 23. They were leaders in their communities who used their positions to take advantage of others rather than help them in their spiritual and physical needs.

There are times when evil and injustice must be confronted—just ask any policeman or soldier. Failure to act will enable the evil to continue impacting lives, communities, even entire countries. Martin Luther King saw the evil of prejudice in our country and bravely took a stand against it. Nelson Mandela looked at apartheid in South Africa and stood courageously against it.

This kind of love is not weak. Taking a stand against evil is never easy. There can be a price to be paid. At the least it can make us unpopular and the target of criticism. It can even bring retribution. Jesus was crucified. Martin Luther King was shot. Nelson Mandela spent twenty-seven years in prison.

Paul addressed another issue of confrontation in Galatians 6:1-2,

*Brothers, if someone is caught in a sin, you who are spiritual should restore him gently. But watch yourself, or you also may be tempted. Carry each other's burdens, and in this way you will fulfill the law of Christ.*

At times confrontational love will require us to extend a helping hand to another believer who has fallen into sin. Compassion and mercy remind us that our goal should be restoration, not judgment and condemnation.

Restoration has the idea of the setting of a broken bone or the mending of nets. Our goal is the binding up of wounds and restoring to spiritual wholeness. It is to be done gently and carefully with the realization we too are flawed and subject to temptation and sin. Strong, compassionate love can have many applications in the home, on the job, in the church and community. It is not easy but requires wisdom. Living for God in our secular world will require us to act with courage and conviction as we confront sin and injustice.

Since love always seeks what is best for others, we will need to ask the question, "How can I act in the best interests of others?" As we learn God's kingdom principles that express love, we can determine how to meet the real needs of those around us. We can be strong and compassionate. It is the way to excel as we live in our flawed world.

## Further study, reflection, and discussion:

1. Use the Scriptures in this chapter for more detailed personal or group study.
2. What are some of the ways we become enablers of those who have problems and dysfunction in their lives?
3. What should be our attitude when exercising tough love?
4. Why is important to consider the consequences of using tough love?
5. How should a believer confront evil and injustice?

22

# When Tough Times Come

*"My God, my God, why have you forsaken me?" cried Jesus in Mark 15:34 quoting from Psalm 22:1*

Dr. James Dobson tells of the loss of four close friends in a plane crash.

The Lord has not revealed His reasons for permitting the plane crash that took the lives of my four friends back in 1987. They were among the finest Christian gentlemen I have ever known. Hugo Schoellkopf was an entrepreneur and an extremely able member of the board of directors for Focus on the Family. George Clark was a bank president and a giant of a man. Dr. Trevor Mabrey was a gifted surgeon who performed nearly half of his operations at no charge to his patients. He was a soft touch for anyone with a financial need. And Creath Davis was a minister and author who was loved by thousands. They were close friends who met regularly to study the Word and assure mutual accountability for what they were learning. I loved these four men.[1]

When we hear of tragedies like this, the human response is to ask the question, "Why?" Those of us who are parents ask this question when a child is diagnosed with a fatal disease. We ask this questions when a son or daughter gives their life, fighting in a faraway place. We ask why when we lose our jobs and the prospect of losing our homes as well. Some of us even seem to have more than our share of pain, trouble, and problems. Specific answers to these and many similar experiences are waiting for us when we get to heaven. In the meantime, how can we as believers cope with the pain and anguish when life becomes difficult?

All of us know tough times are a part of life, but when it happens to us we all ask, "Why is this happening to me?" We also struggle with anger, doubt, and confusion asking "Is God punishing me?" It is important for us to realize that God is not taken by surprise with our questions, anger, doubt, and confusion. These experiences push us out of our comfort zones into the realities of living in a flawed world. The desert experience comes to each of us and impacts those close to us as well.

As believers, how can we move beyond the questioning and negative feelings? It does not come easily. When hard times come, a change in perspective can help us keep from being caught "in between on the misty flats" left to "drift to and fro."

We are reminded in Isaiah 49:13-16 of the words spoken to wayward Israel,

> *Shout for joy, O heavens; rejoice, O earth; burst into song, O mountains! For the Lord comforts his people and will have compassion on his afflicted ones. But Zion said, "The Lord has forsaken me, the Lord has forgotten me." Can a mother forget the baby at her breast and have no compassion on the child she has borne? Though she may forget, I will not forget you! See, I have engraved you on the palms of my hands; your walls are ever before me.*

Many of us have memorized Romans 8:28, "And we know that in all things God works for the good of those who love him, who have been called according to his purpose." While these are words of encouragement, the next question probably is, "If these verses are true, then what are the answers to our questions?"

## The Adversary and Destroyer

First of all, it is important to realize we are in a spiritual battle. While our sinful nature pulls us away from God, it is our enemy, Satan, who seeks to take advantage of our weaknesses and drive us farther from God. His name means adversary, indicating his attitude and posture toward believers. He is called Abaddon (Hebrew) and Apollyon (Greek) in Revelation 9:11. Both mean destroyer, again indicating Satan's intent toward us.

It is essential, then, to realize when we are going through the difficult times of life we can be sure Satan will be there to oppose and seek to destroy us if he can. Study what Satan did to Jesus in Matthew 4 when He fasted forty days in the desert prior to beginning His public ministry. If Satan tempted Jesus, then he will certainly attack us.

Paul gives us a specific list in Ephesians 6:10-18 of the spiritual armor we have to stand firm in the face of Satan's attacks. Verses 10-13 tell us,

> *Finally be strong in the Lord and in his mighty power. Put on the full armor of God so that you can take your stand against the devil's schemes. For our struggle is not against flesh and blood, but against rulers, against the authorities, against the powers of this dark world and against the spiritual forces of evil in the heavenly realms. Therefore put on the full armor of God, so that when the day of evil comes, you may be able to stand your ground. And after you have done everything, to stand.*

We may be sure of this—God will not abandon us. We are not left at the mercy of a ruthless enemy. We may not have all the answers we would like, but we can stand against our adversary who would like to destroy us. God has provided us with the armor and weapons we need to fight the spiritual battle in which we find ourselves.

Moses told the Joshua in Deuteronomy 31:7-8 as he was about to become the leader of the Israelites, "Be strong and courageous, for you must go with this people into the land the Lord swore to their forefathers to give them, and you must divide it among them as their inheritance. The Lord himself goes before you; he will never leave you nor forsake you. Do not be afraid; do not be discouraged." Joshua faced a daunting task like we do at times.

When Jesus gave the great commission in Matthew 28:19-20, He ended it with this statement, "And surely I will be with you always, to the very end of the age." When we face life's difficulties, the sovereign God we serve is always in control. Nothing touches our lives outside the power and presence of God as we seek to follow Him. He is always in control even if we are not.

## Job's Experience

Next, it is helpful to look at the lives of others. Job always comes to mind when we talk about tests and trials. He suffered through the same feelings and questions common to us all. At times he wished he had never been born. He had friends who did not seem to understand what he was experiencing. Satan was determined to destroy him.

Even his wife said to him in Job 2:9-10, "'Are you still holding on to your integrity? Curse God and die!' He replied, 'You are talking like a foolish woman. Shall we not accept good from God, and not trouble?'" His response to his wife indicates a level of maturity that realized God allowed good and bad things to come into his life. He knew that in difficult times, in spite of his questions and confusion, God was still in control. Though he did not fully understand what was happening, he refused to turn from God.

How did Job get to this level of understanding? We are not given a detailed answer to this question. However, Job 1:1 states, "This man was blameless and upright; he feared God and shunned evil." Job was fully committed to serving God with all his heart, soul and mind. We, too, will not always understand what is happening as we go through bad times. The key is to have Job's attitude; to make a heart, soul and mind commitment to serve God in love in the good times and the bad.

## A Test of Commitment

We also are given a measure of wisdom and insight in Moses' challenge to

Israel. He declared in Deuteronomy 8:2, "Remember how the Lord your God led you all the way in the desert these forty years, to humble you and to test you in order to know what was in your heart, whether or not you would keep his commands."

Trials test the commitment of our hearts. They strike at our pride and self-sufficiency. They confront our plans when instead we would like God to bless them by rubber stamping our desires. Tough times cause us to reevaluate those plans. They help us understand that our spiritual welfare is more important than the physical. God, our heavenly Father, is far more interested in what we become spiritually than in making us happy for a short time by just providing what we want. He uses the tools of problems to shape and form us in the image of Christ, something that could not happen any other way. Even though we cannot always see it, God has a plan.

## Jesus' Experience

Hebrews 12:1-13, which was referenced previously, also gives us the New Testament application of dealing with tough times. Take time to read the entire passage. There are two statements to highlight. Verses 2-3 encourage us, "Let us fix our eyes on Jesus, the author and perfecter of our faith, who for the joy set before him endured the cross, scorning its shame, and sat down at the right hand of the throne of God. Consider him who endured such opposition from sinful men, so that you will not grow weary and lose heart."

When life is difficult, remember what Jesus suffered. Mark 15:34 tells us He cried out on the cross, "My God, my God, why have you forsaken me?" Imagine His anguish as He hung on a crude, wooden cross, forsaken by all. His human side even felt abandoned by the Father. He did not deserve any of it, but He chose to take the long range view of what it would accomplish. He did it for you and me.

Next, verse 7 tells us, "Endure hardship as discipline; God is treating you as sons." We have all seen what happens when children are not disciplined. They become selfish, immature and dysfunctional. We also have met those who grew up to be like this as adults. If we are to develop the image of Christ in our lives, God knows we need to be disciplined. This is explained in verse 10, "Our fathers disciplined us for a little while as they thought best; but God disciplines us for our good, that we may share in his holiness."

God has a long range, eternal goal for us to share in His holiness—to make us like His Son, Jesus. He uses tough love to get us there. C. S. Lewis put it this way in his book The Problem of Pain, "God whispers to us in our pleasures, speaks to us in our conscience, but shouts in our pains: it is His megaphone to rouse a deaf world."

# Victory

Even facing death, we too can look beyond our immediate circumstances to the big picture of what God wants to do in our lives. Paul declared in 1 Corinthians 15:55-57, "Where, O death, is your victory? Where, O death is your sting? The sting of death is sin, and the power of sin is the law. But thanks be to God! He gives us the victory through our Lord Jesus Christ." Whether we live or die, we have victory in Christ.

Paul also stated in Philippians 1:21, "For to me, to live is Christ and to die is gain." Death is not a cruel defeat for the believer. It is victory!

And so we have seen some of God's purposes at work in our lives in difficult times. The question remaining is, "How will we choose to respond?" We can choose to become bitter or better. We can rebel in bitterness and anger toward God or we can choose to follow the "high way" by responding in loving commitment to Him. It will not be easy nor is it meant to be. Things that are truly worthwhile are worth the pain and effort to achieve them. Just ask any Olympic athlete.

We can cry out to our Father for help and strength to follow the way of love and surrender. The humanness of Jesus was seen when He prayed in Gethsemane, "Father, if it be possible, may this cup be taken from me. Yet not as I will, but as you will" (Matthew 26:39). We can pray for deliverance, but when God plows deeply in our souls, a prayer we also can pray is, "God, help me to understand what I need to learn in these circumstances."

Even when life is hard, like Job, we can determine to be obedient to Him and be that living sacrifice, surrendering ourselves to His will and way. It is the way Jesus responded in the garden and on the cross. It is how we can respond to God in love. Remember, He will be there! The goal is worth our best effort as we seek to live in excellence in our world.

[1]James Dobson, *When God Doesn't Make Sense* (Wheaton, IL.: Tyndale, 1993), 5-6.

## Further study, reflection, and discussion:

1. Use the Scriptures in this chapter for more detailed personal or group study.
2. Study Psalm 29 and how it applies to difficult times.
3. How do you react when God says no to your plans and desires?
4. How did David react in 2 Samuel 7 when God did not allow him to build the temple?
5. What encouragement for difficult times is given in Hebrews 4:14-16?

23

# Who's the Real Boss?

*Make it your ambition to lead a quiet life, to mind your own business and to work with your hands, just as we told you, so that your daily life may win the respect of outsiders and so that you will not be dependent on anybody* (1 Thessalonians 4:11-12).

Mack, a young seminary student, was at work cleaning an office building at night when he was approached by another worker who said, "Slow down, you are making the rest of us look bad."

John, a committed Christian, was having lunch with his co-workers at a nearby deli. The conversation turned to the secrets of padding their expense accounts. When John objected, he was told that "everbody does it, even the boss."

Susan had just accepted Christ a few weeks earlier. She is an administrative assistant to an executive vice president who told her to tell callers he was not there. He was there; he just didn't want to talk to them.

Sound familiar? These and many other problems confront us when we go to work in our world every day. How are we to deal with such unpleasant and threatening situations? What standards should we use in our workplace?

## The Real Boss

Polls indicate many people do not like their jobs. We long for a job which would give us a sense of accomplishment and satisfaction. Work for many is an endurance contest to see how long we can last. Some are there only to get a paycheck so bills can be paid or some pleasure or hobby pursued. What mindset do we bring to work? Whether we are bosses or employees, this is an area where it may be helpful to change our thinking about our jobs.

Paul wrote to the Christian slaves of his day in Colossians 3:22-24,

*Slaves, obey your earthly masters in everything; and do it, not only when their eye is on you and to win their favor, but with sincerity of heart and reverence for the Lord. Whatever you do, work at it with all your heart, as working for the Lord, not for men. Since you know that you will receive an inheritance from the Lord as a reward. It is the Lord Christ you are serving.*

It is important to understand Paul was not condoning slavery. He was trying to help Christians deal with the realities of the ancient world of work. Thankfully, slavery has been abolished in our culture, but Paul's message is still applicable for us today.

It is essential to remember who the real boss is when we go to work. "It is the Lord Christ you are serving." We work for employers, but our real Boss is Christ Jesus. We may own the business, but we still have a Boss, the Lord Jesus. This puts our workplace in a totally different perspective.

## A Change in Perspective

Our job not only provides us with money for ourselves and our families, but just as importantly it gives us a place where we can live out God's love. It is our personal mission field. Since we are God's spiritual mirrors, what we do each day at work provides us with the opportunity to make God either look good or bad.

There are several important ways this can be done. First, notice Paul said we are to work "with sincerity of heart and reverence for the Lord." He went on to say that work needs to be done "with all your heart." Working with sincerity of heart means we take our work seriously. Working in reverence for the Lord means we are honoring God by the way we work. He is the first One we want to please. This is what Mack, John, and Susan decided would guide them in their jobs. They knew they could not be slackers or cheat and lie.

If Jesus is the real boss, we will begin on time, work hard, and do the best job we can. Coming in late, taking long lunch hours, leaving early, or calling in sick to go to a ball game may be routinely done by others but not those of us who are believers. Cutting corners and working slowly may be done by some but not us. Even when the boss is not there, we choose to work hard because Jesus, the real Boss, does not leave.

Ask any employer and many will say good workers are hard to find. If Jesus is our Boss we can be the kind of workers an employer appreciates—dependable, hard workers who do a good job. At work, we can remember the words of Paul in 1 Corinthians 10:31, "Whatever you do, do it all for the glory of God." It's the way to excel at our work.

Another way we can recognize Jesus as our boss is to work with honesty and integrity. Some corporate security experts estimate that 25% to 40% of all employees steal from their employers, amounting to as much as 50 billion dollars lost a year. Lying and falsifying records is common. This is the environment in which many of us work.

When Paul was carrying an offering for the poor at Jerusalem sent by the church at Corinth, he wrote in 2 Corinthians 8:21, "For we are taking pains to do what is right, not only in the eyes of the Lord, but also in the eyes of men." He wanted to make sure no one would think he misused what had been placed in his care.

What message are we sending when we "borrow" things from work but do not return them? What do our fellow workers think when we spend time on the telephone or computer for personal business or pleasure? What do we do to our testimony for Christ when we pad our expense account or take a fellow worker's customer? It is not always easy to work with integrity and honesty when our fellow workers do not. Some may ridicule and laugh at us. We just need to remember who the boss really is.

## Treat Them Right

Those of us who are employers and managers also need to recognize Jesus as the real Boss. Paul said in Colossians 4:1, "Masters, provide your slaves with what is good and fair, because you know that you have a Master in heaven." It is important to treat employees "with what is good and fair." Treating those under our authority with dignity and respect will go a long way toward creating an environment where most people will want to work hard and do a good job.

You will find these thoughts echoing in Leviticus 19:13, "Do not hold back the wages of a hired man overnight," and Jeremiah 22:13, "Woe to him who builds his palace by unrighteousness, his upper rooms by injustice, making his countrymen work for nothing, not paying them for their labor." It is sad to hear a Christian business person described as "having a sharp pencil" or using his employees just to line his own pockets. As employers or managers, we can set a positive or a negative tone in our work place by the way we treat others.

Tom had just been promoted to manager in a local sports store. He was ambitious and wanted to show his boss he could handle the job. His regional manager had given him some impressive sales goals to reach. He informed his sales staff of these goals and insisted they step up their efforts with customers. At weekly meetings he mentioned by name those who were falling behind. If he thought they were mishandling a customer, he intervened to show them how it should be done. Several employees quit, requiring him to hire new employees.

Six months into his new job, Tom had a job review with the regional manager. Tom was stunned to find his store was falling behind the other stores in his region. He was angry and returned to hold a meeting with his staff. He blasted them, recalling the mistakes they had made. They just were not giving their jobs enough effort. More of the staff quit that week. Six months later, Tom was fired. He blamed it on his workers who had betrayed his hard work.

There seem to be a lot of Toms in the business world. How could we have handled the sales staff to help them reach the company's sales goals? Patrick Lencioni, a management consultant, lists three things employers and managers can do to change the work atmosphere. While not written from a Christian perspective, these three factors resonate with Christian values.

The first is anonymity. He states, "People cannot be fulfilled in their work if they are not known. All human beings need to be understood and appreciated for their unique qualities by someone in a position of authority."[1] Every Christian employer or manager can do much to let employees know they are appreciated. A simple "thanks for your hard work and a good job" often repeated is a start in this direction. Tangible expressions of appreciation are very meaningful to most workers.

The second is irrelevance. He writes, "Everyone needs to know their job matters, to someone, to anyone. Without seeing a connection between the work and the satisfaction of another person or group of people, an employee simply will not find lasting fulfillment."[2] Each worker needs to know what they do is important in the company and to the customers, including the janitor who pushes a broom. As employers and managers, we can help them make that connection.

The last is immeasurement. Lencioni advises, "Employees need to be able to gauge their progress and level of contribution for themselves. They cannot be fulfilled in their work if their success depends on the opinions or whims of another person, no matter how benevolent that person may be."[3]

Most companies practice employee reviews where standards are imposed by management. An even better idea is to help workers develop the criteria for measuring their work. If they help set the standards, they will be more likely to think they are important, not just doing something to make the boss happy.

Occasionally you may have to confront work issues involving dishonesty, safety and injustice. This is where love has to be strong when it is applied. Be willing to "speak the truth in love." Unfortunately, there may be a price to be paid if you are an employee. This is a time to remember who your Boss really is. He can protect you. He provided you with the job you have, and He can provide another one if needed. How you handle these issues as an employer or manager will speak volumes about your values and character. Remember, it is more than the job. It's about people as well. It is about expressing God's love.

Nonbelievers are all around us in the workplace. God has placed us where we work for a purpose. We are there to be a light in a dark place. It is our personal mission field. We do not have to make a big splash or preach. It is a place where we can live out God's love by being good employees who work hard with honesty and integrity.

Those of us who are managers or bosses need to treat employees with dignity and respect. Everyone wants to be appreciated. We can be just the person to do it. Our lives can really count where we work. We need to remember who the Boss really is. It's how we can excel in our jobs.

[1] Patrick Lencioni, *The Three Signs of a Miserable Job* (San Francisco: Jossey-Bass, 2007), 221.
[2] Ibid., 221-222.
[3] Ibid., 222-223.

## Further study, reflection, and discussion:

1. Use the Scriptures in this chapter for more detailed personal or group study.
2. Do you like your job? Why? Why not?
3. Why is your workplace not just a job but a mission field?
4. How can you apply Proverbs 6:6-11; 26:12-16 to your job?
5. If you are a manager or owner, how do you view those who report to you? Are they just employees or something else?
6. Why is it important to treat employees with dignity and respect?

24

# Is Technology of the Devil?

*Computing is not about computers anymore. It is about living.*
—*Nicholas Negroponte*

Thomas J. Watson, the Chairman of the Board of IBM, said in 1943, "I think there is a world market for about five computers." Watson, along with most people of his day, could not envision the rapid development of the information technology age. The world has changed dramatically since then.

Computers are now an integral part of our everyday world. They come in all shapes and sizes in cars, homes, and businesses. We carry them with us as laptops, tablets, phones, and GPS devices. Where a separate device was used for different functions, we now need to buy only one that does it all. Phones are now used as cameras, computers, to listen to music, and watch videos. New products are introduced regularly. People scramble to get the latest and greatest.

As believers, we are a part of this information technology world. The scope of this chapter cannot cover such a vast subject. It is important, however, to bring to this aspect of our culture the same values that guide the rest of our lives. Three areas will be highlighted: the benefits, the dangers, and the responsibilities of believers in the IT age.

## The Benefits

The benefits of the information age are numerous. Quick access to enormous amounts of information is one of the greatest developments. Computers and wireless laptops, iPhones and iPads offer us access from any electronic hotspot or communication satellite.

Pastors, preachers, and educators have available to them vast amounts of study and sermon materials. Videos have changed the way illustrations are presented. We can access a wide variety of websites that offer information and help for church programs. Training sessions are also offered on the Internet. PowerPoint and Smart Boards are routinely used to enhance presentations.

E-books are being offered along with print volumes. Old books and manuscripts are being copied digitally and made available for research. Education of all types and levels, from elementary school to doctorates, is offered online.

New technologies are being developed all the time that will continue to enhance the search for information by us as individuals and by the church.

Sharing information with others is also tremendously improved. Most churches and denominations have developed their own websites. The impact on evangelism and discipleship is obvious, making our follow-up easier and faster. Contact with parishioners and shut-ins has been improved. Prayer requests and testimonies of God's blessings can be routinely posted for the benefit of fellow believers. Many churches record the pastor's sermon and make it available for those who were unable to attend. We no longer need to wait until Sunday to find out what is happening in our churches.

Churches and individuals can keep in touch with missionaries and believers in other countries on an almost daily basis. Email and Skype software have replaced snail-mail (letters sent through the post office) in many countries for communication purposes. We have friends who keep in touch through Skype with their daughter who is a missionary along with her husband and children in Africa. Facebook, Twitter, and other social networking sites are used to keep in contact with saved and unsaved friends alike. All these and much more are the benefits of computers for us and the church.

## The Dangers

Like every manmade invention, computers have their downside. Perhaps the most extreme example was the Korean couple arrested in Seoul for allowing their infant daughter to starve to death. They became obsessed with a virtual daughter named "Anima" in "Prius Online," a popular role-playing game in South Korea. They spent up to twelve hours at a time with "Anima," while not feeding their real daughter.[1] This sad story reminds us that there are many dangers that lurk in the cyber world.

The access to huge amounts of information brings with it the need to sort the true from the false, the good from the bad. Just because someone posts something on a website does not mean it is true or helpful. Parents also need to monitor what their children access online. Chat rooms give sexual predators easy access to children they would never be able to approach on the street. Scam artists, hate groups, cults, and even terrorists lurk in cyber space, seeking to lure the uninformed and vulnerable.

We all have been annoyed by people using their cell phones while driving or shopping. Some people unwisely post improper information and photos using their mobile phones. People have lost their jobs for things they have written in phone texting or posted on Facebook or blogs.

Bullying and attacking others have invaded the world of IT. Pirated software, hackers, identity theft, online dating, and pornography are a part of the computer age. As believers, we need to prepare ourselves when we enter this world.

The amount of time spent on computers is also a concern. People can become addicted in the same way as those who fall victim to drugs or alcohol. Some people spend hours at their computer and neglect those around them. Like the Korean couple, some people retreat into a virtual world that is devoid of human interaction.

We need to remember God's principle of love is relational. A simple email or texting lacks the warmth of our voice or a loving touch and smile. All non-verbal communication is lost. Video cameras help but still fall short of human contact. While technology improves our communication in some ways, it cannot replace our personal touch when we are with someone. We cannot give our loved one a kiss, tousle the heads of children, or stroke the arm of a sick grandparent over the Internet. The news media often show videos of soldiers coming home from overseas to surprise a child in school. We cannot help but have tears in our eyes when the child sees their mom or dad and the hug that follows. Soldiers could never do that on a computer.

## Our Responsibilities

Some have taken the view that computers are of the devil. We tend to think these people are right when our computer crashes. Many new inventions have been met with skepticism. People said the same thing about the radio and later on about television when they were invented.

Some fear computers and refuse to use them. One church organization in the early years of computers petitioned a school district to have their children exempted from computer training. We often fear or ignore what we do not understand. Computers in all varieties are here to stay. We cannot afford to ignore them and we certainly need not fear them. It is important, however, to understand them and their proper use.

As believers, we need to understand our responsibility to use information technology in ways that are consistent with our values. It is worth repeating that it is vitally important for the church to provide the biblical teaching of these values. We need to be inoculated against the dangers mentioned earlier by learning how to live by God's kingdom principles.

These values need to be taught and modeled for our children, along with parental monitoring of their use of modern technology. We are reminded again of Paul's admonition in Ephesians 5:15, "Be very careful, then, how you live—not as unwise but as wise." Again, using God's wisdom we can ask the two questions, "How can I demonstrate my love to God?" and "How can I demonstrate my love to others?"

Computers offer us many benefits as well as dangers. As believers, we can choose to honor God and be obedient to His command to live in integrity and honesty in the information age. Love will motivate us to act in the best interests of others as we interact in the digital world. If we live this way we will build up and strengthen God's kingdom in this fast paced and rapidly changing culture. It is a critical area where we need to excel in our world.

[1]cnn.com/2010/WORLD/asiapcf/03/05/korea.baby.starved/index.html. Accessed June 29, 2011.

## Further study, reflection, and discussion:

1. How much time to you spend on your computer/phone for personal use?
2. Does your use of these devices help or hinder your relationships with family and friends?
3. Do you buy pirated software, music or videos? Why? Why not?
4. What kind of information do you post about yourself on your computer?
5. How would you characterize the programs you access online?
6. How can you use your computer/phone for Christ and His kingdom?

25

# Looking in the Mirror

*Therefore do not let sin reign in our mortal body so that you obey its evil desires. Do not offer the parts of your body to sin, as instruments of wickedness, but rather offer yourselves to God, as those who have been brought to life; and offer the parts of your body to him as instruments of righteousness* (Romans 6:11-13).

What do we think about when we look in a mirror? A few people may be narcissists and admire what they consider to be the perfection of beauty. Most of us, however, think about our flaws like wrinkles, crooked noses, or odd shaped ears. But more importantly, as believers, what do we think God sees? Does He really take a hard look at our physical defects and pass judgment on our lack of beauty or does He enjoy the real beauty of His creation?

When you really think about it, our bodies are marvels of engineering with several trillion cells of staggering complexity. Just look at the intricate working of our brains, hearts, ears, and eyes. Even one cell in our bodies is not just a blob of tissue but is an amazing feat of chemical engineering with a complex DNA code machine. The Bible tells us in Genesis 1:27, "So God created man in his own image, in the image of God he created him; male and female he created them." As believers, we choose to recognize that God is the creator of our amazing bodies. He created us in his own image. We come in a variety sizes, shapes, and colors. We are all unique, special individuals. No one else is quite like you or me.

## An Important Question

The problem we face as believers is our culture tries to tell us our bodies are our own to use as we please. This is the idea behind the pro-abortion movement. It is what happens when God is excluded or denied and doing so leads us down a perilous path.

Obesity and substance abuse in our culture have led to tragic health problems. This raises an important question for believers, "How can we use our bodies to express our love to God?" When answering this question, it is important for us to use biblical principles not the ideas of a culture that excludes God.

Let's take a moment to look at the challenges Moses faced in the Old Testament. Surrounded by ungodly influences, he had to wrestle with a wide variety of issues as he led the Israelites from Egypt to the Promised Land. Among these challenges was the proper use of one's body. Care was taken to distinguish between many things considered to be clean or unclean. Procedures were developed to deal with health issues such as leprosy and other skin diseases. Laws were given prohibiting improper sexual relations. Dietary laws forbid the eating of certain foods from animals considered unclean, such as pigs. The bottom line for all these issues is stated by God for Moses in Leviticus 19:2, "Be holy because I, the Lord your God, am holy." As was noted in an earlier chapter, this principle has not changed for us today. Holiness is still God's standard for how we treat and use our bodies.

## Whose Body Is It?

We have seen that postmodernists tell us there are no standards we have to follow. Truth is whatever we decide works for us. Just have a party. They insist we are to peel away the layers and enjoy all that life has to offer. This includes our bodies and physical pleasures. A quick survey of the news each day shows the sad results of people who misuse their bodies.

Paul takes another approach. He gives us an important principle of holiness concerning our bodies in 1 Corinthians 6:19-20,

> *Do you not know that your body is a temple of the Holy Spirit, who is in you, whom you have received from God? You are not your own; you were bought at a price. Therefore honor God with your body.*

The context of this scripture deals with the problem of men going to prostitutes, but Paul is clear about our bodies. He gives us a broader principle. Our bodies are the temple of the Holy Spirit, who is given to us by God. The price of Jesus' shed blood was paid to make this happen.

This changes the way we view our bodies. It means that we cannot use them any way we please or just because it's the in thing to do. The way we care for our bodies is an important way we can honor and glorify God and express our love to Him. This is a game changing idea that impacts our lives in so many ways.

## The Right Focus

Molly was having a tough time with her daughter, Amy, who had just become a teenager. Amy wanted all the trendy clothes to keep up with her friends. Peer pressure is a powerful influence in teenagers' lives. The fact that she was noticing boys did not help the matter either. What's a mother to do?

Peter gave some good advice to the women of his day in 1 Peter 3:3-4,

> *Your beauty should not come from outward adornment, such as braided hair and the wearing of gold jewelry and fine clothes. Instead, it should be that of your inner self, the unfading beauty of a gentle and quiet spirit, which is of great worth in the sight of God.*

The principle of holiness for us is to focus on our inner beauty. This does not mean we should neglect or forget about our outward appearance. But while we want to look our best, do we want to get caught up in the attitude of our culture that values the outside and ignores the inner beauty of godly character?

Paul also spoke to the outward appearance in 1 Timothy 2:9-10 where he said to the women of his day,

> *I also want women to dress modestly, with decency and propriety, not with braided hair or gold or pearls or expensive clothes, but with good deeds, appropriate for women who profess to worship God.*

Paul addresses this specifically to women, however, some tend to get caught up in the details of what Paul said to them and miss an important, underlying principle that applies to us all. Men today would do well to listen to the advice of Paul and Peter as well.

It is the principle of modesty which Paul qualifies with two words, decency and propriety. The meaning is that of reverence and discipline, not brazen self display. We live in a very fashion conscious world where men are just as vain as women about their appearance. Modesty is scarcely a consideration. The more revealing and tantalizing the clothes, the more in demand they are. You do not want to be accused of looking dull and old school.

The right label in any garment is also a coveted prize by many when shopping. Jewelry and many other accessories are must haves if we are to be in vogue. The more expensive, the better it is, or so we are told by advertising. We need to wrestle with the question, "How much is enough?" Can we justify the amount we spend just to look good? Are we accepting our cultures standards of how to look or are we seeking to glorify God in modesty and decency?

It is a matter of priorities. How much time do we spend trying to look just right as compared to the time we spend on our spiritual growth and development? What are we emphasizing in our lives? Is it how we look or is it living a life that is pleasing and glorifying to God?

## Staying in the Boundaries

We face not only the issues of our outward appearance, but what we do with our bodies. God has made us with basic physical needs and desires such as food, drink, and sex. Our culture offers us a smorgasbord of ways to satisfy these physical pleasures. Just peel back the layers of the onion. The problem we must confront is using these things within the boundaries God has set for us. Should we do things to and with our bodies just because our culture considers them the "thing to do"?

Paul the apostle realized these issues in his own life. He compared the believer's life to an athlete's race stating in 1 Corinthians 9:24-27,

> *Do you not know that in a race all the runners run, but only one gets the prize? Run in such a way as to get the prize. Everyone who competes in the games goes into strict training. They do it to get a crown that will not last; but we do it to get a crown that will last forever. Therefore I do not run like a man running aimlessly; I do not fight like a man beating the air. No, I beat my body and make it my slave so that after I have preached to others, I myself will not be disqualified for the prize.*

Keeping his body under control was Paul's way of staying in God's boundaries. It is a good way for us to live as well. What are our goals in life? Are we centered on the temporary things that give our bodies pleasure or are we disciplining ourselves to run the race to win the prize God set for us?

When we are tempted to do something to or with our bodies we can ask the question, "Am I just identifying with the culture around me or am I seeking to honor God?" When we sit down for a meal, ask ourselves the question, "How can I honor God?" We may need to do some push-a-ways as well as some push-ups. When we go to our closet, we can ask the question, "How can I honor God by what I am choosing to wear?" We may need to throw away some inappropriate clothes. "How can I honor God with my body?" is the question love asks. When we look in the mirror, what do we see—our body or God's temple?

These are the questions Molly needs to teach Amy to ask. Amy needs to learn it is not just about how she looks on the outside but how she views her body as God's temple. While she can still look good, it is important for her to learn the truth about her body.

As believers it is important to take personal responsibility for our bodies and search God's Word for guidance on how we should use it. Again, James 1:5 promises us, "If any of you lacks wisdom, he should ask God, who gives generously to all without finding fault, and it will be given him." We can use our Guide Book. God will show us how to express our love by honoring Him with His temple, our bodies. We want to look good, but do so in modesty. It's the way to excel in world that focuses only on how we look.

## Further study, reflection, and discussion:

1. Use the Scriptures in this chapter for more detailed personal or group study.
2. What does Romans 6:15-23 teach us about our bodies?
3. What are some of the ways our culture captures us in our clothing, our appearance, our diet?
4. How much of our culture should we copy as believers in our clothing, appearance and diet?
5. Define modesty and moderation from a Christian perspective?

# 26

# Managers and Groundskeepers

*For six years sow your fields, and for six years prune your vineyards and gather your crops. But in the seventh year the land is to have a sabbath of rest, a sabbath to the Lord* (Leviticus 25:3-4).

April 20, 2010 will long be remembered for the explosion that caused the Deepwater Horizon oil spill in the Gulf of Mexico. Lives were lost and people injured. An ecological disaster of enormous proportions developed. Thousands of people along the Gulf saw their jobs disappear and their futures clouded and changed.

March 11, 2011 was marked in Japan by an offshore earthquake and tsunami that wreaked havoc on the Fukushima Daiichi nuclear power plant. Radiation severely hampered relief efforts to reach survivors and eventually spread around the world. Like other nuclear disasters, the effects will last for many years.

Older people will remember the pollution of the Love Canal in Niagara Falls, New York, where twenty-one tons of toxic wastes were buried. Problems were brought to the attention of the public in the late 1970s. Schools and homes had been built near the site. Severe health problems had developed among residents including miscarriages and birth defects. Today the site is vacant. Homes and schools have long ago been demolished.

## A Variety of Attitudes

As believers, what is our reaction toward these events? They raise the question of what our attitude should be toward the physical world in which we live. Ecology is a broad area encompassing many different areas of science. It is not the purpose of this chapter to enter the debate of the scientific issues. Most of us lack the expertise to know and understand the details that are involved. These problems are also complicated because of the philosophical and political climate that influences the interpretation of the facts.

Some people think the physical world is there to be used any way they want as long as it pleases and profits them. People like this have long pillaged the land and its creatures, leaving in their wake pollution and animal extinction.

The news media reminds us from time to time of animal cruelty from cock and dog fighting or puppy mills.

Others have gone to the opposite extreme and treat the physical world with a god-like spiritual reverence by worshiping mother nature. Some have climbed trees to protect the forests. Some have used violence to advance these views by attacking research facilities that use animals.

Just because others have views about the environment that are not consistent with the Bible, however, does not mean we can turn a deaf ear to the way we use the resources and treat the creatures of our world. There are several truths in the Bible we need to understand that speak to the way we interact with our physical world and its creatures.

## A Good Creation

The first idea is found in Genesis 1:1, "In the beginning God created the heavens and the earth." Psalm 24:1 also states, "The earth is the Lord's, and everything in it, the world, and all who live in it.

Five times in Genesis 1 we find this statement, "And God saw that it was good." Verse 31 summarizes by declaring, "God saw all that he had made, and it was very good." These verses make it clear, God created the heavens and the earth. It is valued because He created it. It all belongs to Him. Note that He declared His creation to be "very good." This lets us know we need to be careful how we use what God has called very good.

## Good Managers

Secondly, we need to understand our relationship to God and His creation. Genesis 1:28 tells us that God said to man, "Be fruitful and increase in number; fill the earth and subdue it. Rule over the fish of the sea and the birds of the air and over every living creature that moves on the ground." Genesis 2:15 continues by adding, "The Lord took the man and put him in the Garden of Eden to work it and take care of it." These verses indicate that man was given a managerial role over God's creation.

Our status has not changed in relation to our physical world. God expects us to take care of what he has entrusted to our care. The opening verses quoted at the beginning of this chapter, from Leviticus 25:3-4, reinforced this principle to the Israelites. We may think we and the bank own our homes, property, or businesses. However, everything has been created by God and given to us to manage properly for His glory. We also are to treat all of God's creatures in a way consistent with His mandate.

Most of us do not notice groundskeepers except when the lawn mower comes within hearing even though their work is important. Those of us who golf appreciate a well-kept golf course. When we go into a place of business that is shabby and rundown, we wonder what goes on inside. As believers we do not want people to wonder about our commitment to be good groundskeepers of our world.

## A Broken Command

Next, it is important to understand that this trust to manage God's creation has been broken. Genesis 3 records the sad story of Adam and Eve disobeying God's command not to eat from the tree of the knowledge of good and evil. They ate the fruit and came under God's judgment. Mankind became sinners. The ground was cursed because of their disobedience and mismanagement. Some have mistakenly viewed this curse on the land as a reason to neglect the environment. Just the opposite is true.

Adam and Eve teach us an important lesson. There is a heavy price to pay when we disobey and mismanage the creation God has entrusted to our care. Unfortunately, some today continue the same pattern of Adam and Eve. We are sinners and we rebel against the way God wants us to live. So if we misuse the environment and its creatures, it is safe to say we will reap the results of our own free choices. The problem is that innocent people can be tragically affected by our misdeeds. Love Canal is a graphic reminder of this.

God has created laws that govern the way nature functions. There are very powerful forces at work in these processes. Just listen to the crackle of lightning in a thunderstorm or look at the power of ocean waves pounding against a rocky shore. When we fail to respect and care for God's creation, we can unleash these forces at our own peril. What happened in the Gulf of Mexico and more recently in Japan's nuclear facility at Fukushima dramatically remind us of this.

## A New Creation

Lastly, though sin has marred our world, Romans 8:20-21 informs us,

*For the creation was subjected to frustration, not by its own choice, but by the will of the one who subjected it, in hope that the creation itself will be liberated from its bondage to decay and brought into the glorious freedom of the children of God.*

Isaiah 65:17 finds God declaring, "Behold, I will create new heavens and a new earth." This is our hope. One day not only our bodies will be transformed but the whole of God's creation. Until that day, let us manage the world God has given us with care and integrity.

As believers, we will want to be informed of the best way to care for those specific areas of God's creation that have been given to us. Again, Ephesians 5:15 teaches us, "Be very careful, then, how you live—not as unwise but as wise."

Until God creates all things new, His creation deserves the very best we can give. It may be as simple as placing our trash and recycling bins at the end of the drive way or as complex as becoming a scientist who studies the environment. Caring for God's creation is one of the ways we express our love to Him and bring glory to His name as we live in our world. God's world deserves our excellence.

## Further study, reflection, and discussion:

1. Use the Scriptures in this chapter for more detailed personal or group study.
2. How does man misuse the creation God has called good?
3. What does Psalm 8 teach us about our responsibility to God's creation?
4. How can we become better informed about using the resources of God's creation?
5. What changes in lifestyle can we make to be more responsible managers of God's creation?

27

# A Step Further

*The Spirit of the Lord is on me, because he has anointed me to preach good news to the poor. He has sent me to proclaim freedom for the prisoners and recovery of sight for the blind, to release the oppressed, to proclaim the year of the Lord's favor* (Luke 4:18-19).

At the end of the war with Japan in World War II, something amazing happened when the POW camps for Allied prisoners were located. Many prisoners had already died from abuse, disease, and lack of food. American planes dropped food to the remaining prisoners who had been starved and cruelly brutalized.

So much food was air-dropped that the prisoners at Naoetsu took some of it to the Japanese people around the camps who were also starving.[1] It is a remarkable story of giving to those in need in terrible times. It stirs our hearts. It gives vivid meaning to Jesus' command to "love your enemies" in Matthew 5:44.

## A Biblical Mandate

Jesus taught us in Matthew 25:34-36,

*Come, you who are blessed by my Father; take your inheritance, the kingdom prepared for you since the creation of the world. For I was hungry and you gave me something to eat, I was thirsty and you gave me something to drink, I was a stranger and you invited me in, I needed clothes and you clothed me, I was sick and you looked after me, I was in prison and you came to visit me.*

Then Jesus made an important statement in verse 40, "I tell you the truth, whatever you did for one of the least of these brothers of mine, you did for me." Jesus was telling us that helping those in need is the same as helping God Himself.

Jesus' teaching was not new. He was drawing on something the people of His day already knew. Moses had taught a similar idea in Leviticus 19:9-10,

*When you reap the harvest of your land, do not reap to the very edges of your field or gather the gleanings of your harvest. Do not go over your vineyard a second time or pick grapes that have fallen. Leave them for the poor and alien. I am the Lord your God.*

This is the same chapter in Leviticus where Jesus took His answer to the Pharisee in Matthew 22:39, "Love your neighbor as yourself." Loving our neighbor includes the poor and the alien, those who are on the margins of life as we know it.

## Comfortable Christianity

Tom and Alice are believers who faithfully attend their church. Alice teaches the girls' club on Wednesday evenings. Tom is a member of the local Christian motorcycle fellowship. They read their Bibles and pray most days. They even pay their tithes and occasionally put a check in the offering to support missionaries. They give a few cans of food to the local food drive and some old clothes to the local homeless shelter. They are good people, respected by those who know them.

Something is missing, however. When they read Scriptures such as Luke 4:18-19 (see above), like so many Christians, they give it a spiritual meaning and apply it only to the unsaved. They fail to realize that Jesus was talking about real people with real needs that could be met if believers would put the Gospel to work in practical ways.

Tom and Alice dramatize the issue for many of us today who live fairly comfortable, routine lives but ignore the pressing needs of people whom we pass everyday on the way to work. Too many of us remain uninformed of the serious social problems here and in other countries that keep people in extreme poverty and even slavery of various kinds. Those of us like Tom and Alice need to take a step further in our walk with Christ.

Richard Stearns, the president of World Vision, describes his introduction in Rakai, Uganda, to the realities of poverty, sin, and suffering.

His name was Richard, the same as mine. I sat inside his meager thatch hut, listening to his story, told through the tears of an orphan whose parents had died of AIDS. At thirteen, Richard was trying to raise his two younger brothers by himself in this small shack with no running water, electricity, or even beds to sleep in. There were no adults in their lives. There was no one to care for them, feed them, love them, or teach them how to become men. There was no one to hug them either, or tuck them in at night. Other than his siblings, Richard was alone, as no child should be. I try to picture my own children abandoned in this kind of deprivation, fending for themselves without parents, and I cannot."[2]

Giving a few cans of food in a local food drive and some old clothing to a local homeless shelter are commendable acts of charity. But are they enough? The Gospel must have a much greater impact than this in our enormously needy world. There are Richards all over the world in poverty, some even slaves in the world sex trade. Unfortunately, some of us have been reluctant to become involved in what is called the social gospel. The history of social involvement by Christians has been distorted by liberal theologians who have emphasized only that aspect of the Jesus' teachings. This was seen by conservative believers as neglecting the spiritual side of salvation.

The two sides have chosen to reject the other's emphasis and methods. Both sides have erred by creating a false division between the sacred and the social applications of the Gospel. The Bible and history do not support this separation.

## Changing Our World

Reading the command in Genesis 1:28 to Adam to "be fruitful and increase in number, fill the earth and subdue it," should cause us to pause and consider the implications of what God said. Mankind did not remain farmers for long but began to gather in groups and then in towns, which developed into larger societies and cultures. The command to subdue must include not only the ground for growing crops but the cultures that developed as a result of that first harvest.

The quote used to open this chapter was made by Jesus when He read from Isaiah 61:1-2 in the synagogue in Nazareth. This passage cannot help but convince us that Jesus was talking about more than just the souls of the poor, the prisoners, the blind, and the oppressed. Other passages resonate with the same message. Jesus teaching in Matthew 5:13-16 that we are to be salt and light means more than just living good moral lives. Our actions to change our world are included as well.

The Lord's Prayer in Matthew 6:9-13 has been recited countless times by believers and non-believers alike. Jesus taught us to pray, "Your kingdom come, your will be done on earth as it is in heaven." He clearly meant the coming of God's kingdom was not to be some far off future event, but it was to have an immediate impact on earth. Since the kingdom of God is within us as believers, it is meant change to us, and we then are to change the world. As believers we are not meant to be containers of the Gospel but conduits through which the Gospel in all its implications flows to the world around us.

St. Patrick as a boy was captured in 401 A.D. and brought from Britain to

Ireland as a slave. He spent several years as a shepherd where he faced his lonely isolation and began praying. It was this experience that drew him to God. He eventually escaped and returned home. He soon realized that God wanted him to return to Ireland, the land of his slavery. After a period of theological training, Patrick returned to face the warlike, primitive, and pagan culture of Ireland. Ireland was forever changed.

William Wilberforce was a member of the British parliament who worked tirelessly for twenty-three years to abolish the slave trade in the British Empire. He along with others worked from 1784 to 1807 when the Slave Trade Act was passed. A few days after Wilberforce died in 1833, parliament passed an emancipation act, freeing all slaves throughout the British Empire. What made the difference? Wilberforce became an evangelical Christian in 1784. This dramatically changed his life and he then helped change the British Empire.

More modern times give us other examples like Martin Luther King, who gave his life in changing a segregated United States. Mother Theresa entered the poverty of India and captured the attention of the world with her service to the poor and sick who were locked in abject poverty in a culture controlled by a caste system. She dared to reach out and touch the untouchables.

What can we do to change our world? We have seen that we must first be changed ourselves by making a commitment to follow Christ and His command to love God and love others. However, we cannot stop with just changing ourselves. We must preach the Gospel to every creature and seek to build the kingdom of God in a broken world.

As Jesus said, this must include the poor, the prisoners, the blind, and the oppressed. He indicated that was what He came to do. We may be tempted to react by saying, "I'm not a St. Patrick or a Mother Theresa." And we may be right. However, we must not hide behind this and not do what God is calling us to do where we are.

Chuck Colson and Nancy Pearcey tell the true story of Danny Croce who found himself in prison after running over a police officer while in a drug-induced haze. Danny was a boxer who was able to defend himself against the attacks of fellow prisoners. What he could not defend against were the nightmares from the accident that ruled the night and ruined his sleep.

A fellow inmate invited him to a group for vehicular-homicide prisoners. One person asked Danny if he ever prayed to God. Spurred by this question, Danny prayed for God to let him sleep. He did sleep that night for the first time in months. He later visited the prison chaplain who encouraged him to confess his sins and invite Christ into his heart as Lord. He followed through in his cell. He slept through the night that night and each night afterward.

Danny finally finished his prison sentence. Ten years later, after attending

Wheaton College on a scholarship from the Charles W. Colson Scholarship for ex-offenders, he returned to the prison where he had served his sentence as the new prison chaplain.[3]

Danny responded to a need he knew well. His time in prison had prepared him for his new job. He answered the call of God by using his experiences and gifts to help change the lives of other prisoners like himself. He was married and had children and could have settled into a comfortable life. But he took a step further to help change his world.

What about us? What can we do? God has placed us in strategic places right where we are. What is God calling us to do? Some of us may be a mechanics. How can we impact our work place? Some of us may be policemen. How can we change our world with Christian values? Some of us may be doctors. How can we help the world of medicine and science to be better? Some of us are stay-at-home moms. How can moms influence the world of their husbands, children, families, and friends? Some of us are retired. As a retired person, I have found sitting on the sidelines to be dull and boring. There is a world of needs around us that we can seek to change. After all, we have lots of experience. Which one will we choose?

Believers are everywhere. We all have gifts and abilities. Opportunities to build God's kingdom abound. God is calling us are where we are to change our world for the kingdom of God.

That is what Barbara Vogel did with her fourth grade class in 1998 in Aurora, Colorado. She shared with them about the civil war in the Sudan where Christians were being captured and sold as slaves by neighboring Muslims. After their initial shock where some even cried, the students wanted to do something to help. So they formed a group they named STOP for Slavery That Oppresses People. They partnered with Christian Solidarity, an organization that redeems slaves by buying them back from their owners. Some of the students were poor themselves, but they saved their allowances, sold lemonade, T-shirts, and old toys. They raised enough to free one hundred fifty people from slavery.

They were not satisfied with that and sent letters to newspapers and public leaders. A homeless man living in his car sent his last $100. A class of handicapped children held a bake sale. A truck driver spread the story everywhere he went. Before the end of the school year they had raised over $50,000. More than five thousand slaves were set free and returned to their families. Where did this begin? Barbara Vogel is a committed Christian who put feet and hands to her faith in a public school that does not allow teachers to talk about Jesus from a faith perspective.[4]

All of us can pray. Most of us can give to support those who go. Some of us will hear God's voice saying, "Go!" He says to all of us, "Take a step further!" All of us can find a way to be the hands and feet of Jesus to our broken world. We can bring good news to the poor; proclaim freedom to prisoners; sight for the blind; freedom for the oppressed.

There are many faith-based organizations and programs across our country and around the world worthy of our support. Each of us can take that step further. It is the way to live out God's love to a world of need. It is how we can fulfill the line in the Lord's Prayer, "Your kingdom come." What a way to bring excellence to our world!

[1]Laura Hillenbrand, *Unbroken* (New York: Random House, 2010), 315.
[2]Richard Stearns, *The Hole in Our Gospel* (Nashville: Thomas Nelson, 2009), 7.
[3]Charles Colson and Nancy Pearcey, *How Now Shall We Live?* (Wheaton, IL.: Tyndale, 1999), 283-292.
[4]Ibid., 415-416.

## Further study, reflection, and discussion:

1. Use the Scriptures in this chapter for more detailed personal or group study.
2. Write out a plan to impact your needy world.
3. What happened in Acts 2:44-45; 4:32-35; 6:1-6?
4. What did Paul urge the Corinthian believers to do in 1 Corinthians 16:1-4?
5. What do we learn from James 2:14-18 about helping others?
6. Why is wisdom so important in helping others?

28

# When We Get Dusty

*As a father has compassion on those who fear him, so the Lord has compassion on those who fear him: for he knows how we are formed, he remembers we are dust* (Psalm 103:13-14).

Remember Sophie from the chapter "Don't fake It"? She was the one who embezzled money from the local little league. She and her family eventually had to move to another area of the country to escape the notoriety of what she had done. She and Mike, her husband, were able to save their marriage by going for marriage counseling. Mike was able to find a job so their lives seemed to be getting back on the right path. They even began attending a local church.

Sophie, however, was reluctant to make friends. Suppose someone discovered what she had done. Embarrassment and guilt hung over her like a cloud of gloom. She struggled spiritually as well. How could God ever forgive her for the terrible harm she had caused, especially to her family?

## All of Us Experience Failure

It would be easy to be judgmental and declare that Sophie would reap what she had sown. Actually, Sophie had already endured some bitter reaping. How could she find her way back to God? What would we do?

Most of us will never steal like Sophie, but that does not mean we have a clean slate either. The verses from Psalm 103 that introduced this chapter tell us God remembers we are dust. This means He understands our weakness and frailty better than we think. One preacher said it well, "We all get dusty at times." Isaiah 53:6 puts it this way, "We all, like sheep have gone astray, each of us has turned to his own way."

The honest truth is we all stumble and fall in our walk with God. David sinned with Bathsheba. Peter denied Jesus three times. Before his conversion Paul stood as a Pharisee and watched Stephen stoned to death. Mark deserted Paul on one of his journeys to spread the gospel. Living in love toward God and others is not always a smooth and easy path. None of us gets it right all the time.

We face three main obstacles: our own sinful nature, a culture that pulls us every day toward a secular lifestyle, and the devil who seeks our destruction. These operate hand-in-glove causing us to fall short of our spiritual goals and beat us down in defeat. The real question is the same as Sophie's, "How can we find our way back to God?"

## A God of Grace and Compassion

How we deal with our failures is vitally important. It is easy to give up, declaring, "What's the use!" Sophie faced this issue, but deep inside her desire to get back to God tugged at her heart. If we were counseling Sophie, what would we say to her? Some people view God as the Judge, ready to pass sentence and pound us in judgment. Sophie struggled with this. She had a poor relationship with her father that affected her understanding of God. As a pastor, I have counseled many believers over the years who struggled with this same issue. Some would not even take communion because they did not feel worthy. This changed for them when they came to realize they could take communion because Jesus was their worthiness.

What is God like? Our culture wants to emphasize God's love and ignore His righteousness and justice. Understanding the relationship of these aspects of God's nature is critical to have a healthy view of God. Briefly stated, God in His wisdom has chosen to temper His justice and righteousness with His love. He would be justified to punish us based on our sins, but He has chosen not to do so when we turn to Him in repentance. He sent Christ to take the punishment we deserved when He died on the cross.

A good example of this is found in God's dealings with the nation of Israel. Over and over in the Old Testament we read of the Jews sinning. When they repented and turned to God, He forgave them. Even when they were punished, God waited patiently for them to repent and turn to Him. The story of Israel is really our story and it was Sophie's story as well. She found a local pastor who helped her overcome her flawed views of God as a condemning judge. He was able to share with her from the Bible what God is really like.

Psalm 103:8-14 tells us how God responds when we repent,

*The Lord is compassionate and gracious, slow to anger, abounding in love. He will not always accuse, nor does he harbor his anger forever; he does not treat us as our sins deserve or repay us according to our iniquities. For as high as the heavens are above the earth, so great is his love for those who fear him; as far as the east is from the west, so far has he removed our transgressions from us.*

The opening verses at the beginning of this chapter complete the thought, "As a father has compassion on his children, so the Lord has compassion on those who fear him; for he knows how we are formed, he remembers that we are dust."

God's love and grace is the reason Jesus came to die on a cross for our sins. John 3:16-17 states this eloquently,

*For God so loved the world that he gave his one and only Son, that whoever believes in him shall not perish but have eternal life. For God did not send his Son into the world to condemn the world, but to save the world through him.*

We can substitute our names in these verses and make it personal.

## The Path Back to God

This, then, is the understanding of God we need when we stumble, fall, and end up dusty. We can repent of our sins and turn to God. First John 1:9 assures us, "If we confess our sins, he is faithful and just and will forgive us our sins and purify us from all unrighteousness." Notice the encompassing words "all unrighteousness." What Sophie had done was an egregious act, but it, too, is included in the phrase "all unrighteousness." It's true for each of us. God forgives all our sins when we repent.

First John 2:1 encourages us, "But if anybody does sin, we have one who speaks to the Father in our defense—Jesus Christ, the Righteous One." Jesus not only died on the cross for our sins, but, like a defense attorney in court, He speaks to God the Father on our behalf. Think of it, we have someone pleading our case 24/7. His name is Jesus, and He is there when we get dusty.

And don't forget, we have the promise of the Holy Spirit as well—the One called alongside to help. He also will be there 24/7 to help, teach, and guide. It is a journey where we walk each day as a "living sacrifice" moving forward in God's love.

When the impact of the true picture of God grace, compassion, and mercy dawned in Sophie's heart and mind, the cloud of guilt was lifted. Tears trickled down her cheeks. Her face lit up with a huge smile. She finally felt free from the bondage of her past.

We too can experience the wonderful redeeming love of God revealed in His grace, compassion, and mercy. When we fail to live in love, we can repent and open our lives to God. The scars of our past may remain, but our spirits can soar as we are freed from our guilt. He is the one who can dust us off and clean up our lives by His grace. Becoming dusty does not mean the journey has to end. Through God's grace and forgiveness we can stay on the path to excellence in our world.

## Further study, reflection, and discussion:

1. Use the Scriptures in this chapter for more detailed personal or group study.
2. Even though we know God has forgiven us, why do we find it hard to forgive ourselves?
3. How should we react to people like Sophie?
4. What should we do when our sin impacts others?

29

# Enter the "High Way"

Our world is hungry for genuinely changed people. Leo Tolstoy observes, "Everybody thinks of changing humanity and nobody thinks of changing himself." Let us be among those who believe that the inner transformation of our lives is a goal worthy of our best effort.
—*Richard Foster*

Most of us know C. S. Lewis as the writer of *The Chronicles of Narnia*. Three movies have been made from his book to the delight of many children (and not a few adults). What many may not know is that Lewis was a committed Christian. It is not hard to figure out who the lion, Aslan, represents.

Lewis, an Oxford University don and scholar of medieval literature, was greatly influenced by the writings of G. K. Chesterton and was close friends with J. R. R. Tolkien who wrote *The Lord of the Rings* trilogy. He declared his faith in Christ on October 1, 1931 when he wrote to a friend, "I have just passed on from believing in God to definitely believing in Christ—in Christianity."[1]

Lewis was a prolific writer and broadcast his views on Christianity on the BBC during World War II. His writings continue to have an enormous impact on the Christian community. A study of his works reveals that Lewis held friendships and relationships in high regard. His book *The Four Loves* shows us that he understood the importance of modeling God's love in our lives. He understood the importance of entering and following the "high way." When we read the *Chronicles of Narnia* or watch the movies, we find the "high way" embedded in the stories.

While few of us will match the accomplishments of C. S. Lewis, that is not the point. We do not have the same gifts and abilities, but as Lewis wrote, we all can express God's love to those around us. We live in many separate places and there are a wide variety things we can do as believers to impact our world. Like C. S. Lewis, we can leave a legacy of love. Most of us will never write a book, but the effect we have in our daily endeavors will be determined by how well we love God and others. That was Paul's main point in 1 Corinthians 13. What motivates us makes a tremendous difference.

The poem at the beginning of this book challenged us to seek the "high way." The choice is up to each believer to make a heart, soul, and mind commitment to love God and his/her neighbor. This is the "high way." It is how we can excel in our world. Our choices will affect our relationships, how we talk and act, where we go, and how we treat our bodies and manage God's creation.

We can find out how to do this by studying our Guide Book, the Bible. It is a treasure trove which we can mine to access the riches of God's wisdom for how we should live. We can start with the two basic questions: "How can I express my love to God?" and "How can I express my love to others?"

Paul knew what it was like to live for God in his world. He was not an out of touch idealist who saw life through distorted lenses. Remember how he declared his commitment in Philippians 3:13-14, "Forgetting what is behind and straining toward what is ahead, I press on toward the goal to win the prize for which God has called me heavenward in Christ Jesus." He pressed on in his commitment to follow God in spite of his own weaknesses and the opposition of others. He knew the goal was worth the effort.

Living in love is richly rewarding in this life and lays the foundation for the glorious future that awaits us when Christ returns. Colossians 3:12-14 sums it up well, "Therefore, as God's chosen people, holy and dearly loved, clothe yourselves with compassion, kindness, humility, gentleness and patience. Bear with each other and forgive whatever grievances you may have against one another. Forgive as the Lord forgave you. And over all these virtues put on love, which binds them all together in perfect unity."

Let's summarize what we have learned. We live in an off-key culture that seeks to hold us captive to its beliefs; but as believers, we have an important mission in life. We do not have to remain in captivity and be left "in between on the misty flats" to "drift to and fro." We have been called and chosen to be a part of God's kingdom to represent Him right where we are.

Living in love toward God and others is at the heart of living in God's kingdom. It is the key to bringing glory to God and becoming holy like Jesus Himself. It is the gate to a different path. We can make a difference and impact our world for God's great kingdom. We can make that commitment to enter God's "high way" today. It is how we are meant to excel in our world.

[1] Alan Jacobs, *The Narnian* (HarperSanFrancisco, 2005), 150.

## Further study, reflection, and discussion:

1. Use the Scriptures in this chapter for more detailed personal or group study.
2. What does Paul's prayer in Ephesians 3:14-19 tell us about the entering the "high way?"
3. What can we learn from 2 Peter 1:3-11 about the "high way?"

# About the Author

Born and raised in Florida, James (Jim) Barco accepted Christ as a young boy. Early on he began to feel a tug in his heart toward ministry. After high school, he began his training to fulfill this call by attending Southeastern University in Lakeland, Florida. He was graduated with a Bachelor of Arts in theology. Feeling the need for further training, he attended Gordon-Conwell Theological Seminary and received a Master of Divinity. It was there he met and married Camille. They are the parents of two children and have seven grandchildren.

He received a Master of Education degree from Massachusetts College of Liberal Arts and taught in Elementary education for three years. He was ordained as a minister of the Assemblies of God in 1968. Jim, along with Camille, served four churches spanning 22 years. He served in numerous leadership positions at a district/state level. He has written many unpublished Bible study lessons, which were used in the churches he served.

In 1991, he entered a different ministry at Valley Forge Christian College where he was the college registrar for almost 15 years. During that time he also was an adjunct instructor in numerous college courses.

Retiring in 2006, Jim and Camille live in southeastern Pennsylvania where they remain active in local church ministry. It was here he felt the urge to write down his thoughts for his grandchildren. As he wrote, it began to occur to him others might also benefit from what he wanted to say. These thoughts grew to become this book.

You can contact Jim and Camille at excel.in.life52@gmail.com.